Mastering Your Adult ADHD

Mastering Your Adult ADHD

A COGNITIVE-BEHAVIORAL TREATMENT PROGRAM

Therapist Guide

Steven A. Safren • Carol A. Perlman

Susan Sprich • Michael W. Otto

UNIVERSITY PRESS

2005

OXFORD
UNIVERSITY PRESS

Oxford University Press, Inc., publishes works that further
Oxford University's objective of excellence
in research, scholarship, and education.

Oxford   New York
Auckland   Cape Town   Dar es Salaam   Hong Kong   Karachi
Kuala Lumpur   Madrid   Melbourne   Mexico City   Nairobi
New Delhi   Shanghai   Taipei   Toronto

With offices in
Argentina   Austria   Brazil   Chile   Czech Republic   France   Greece
Guatemala   Hungary   Italy   Japan   Poland   Portugal   Singapore
South Korea   Switzerland   Thailand   Turkey   Ukraine   Vietnam

Copyright © 2005 by Oxford University Press, Inc.

Published by Oxford University Press, Inc.
198 Madison Avenue, New York, New York 10016

www.oup.com

Oxford is a registered trademark of Oxford University Press

Library of Congress Cataloging-in-Publication Data
Mastering your adult ADHD—therapist guide : a cognitive-behavioral treatment
program / Steven A. Safren ... [et al.].
p.   cm.
Includes bibliographical references.
ISBN-10: 0-19-518818-7
ISBN-13: 978-0-19-518818-9
1. Attention-deficit disorder in adults. 2. Cognitive therapy. I. Safren, Steven A.
RC552.P67M364 2005
616.85´8906—dc22   2005001269

9 8 7 6 5 4 3 2 1

Printed in the United States
on acid-free paper

About Treatments That Work™

Stunning developments in health care have taken place over the last several years, but many of our widely accepted interventions and strategies in mental health and behavioral medicine have been brought into question by research evidence as not only lacking benefit but perhaps inducing harm. Other strategies have been proven effective using the best current standards of evidence, resulting in broad-based recommendations to make these practices more available to the public. Several recent developments are behind this revolution. First, we have arrived at a much deeper understanding of pathology, both psychological and physical, which has led to the development of new, more precisely targeted interventions. Second, our research methodologies have improved substantially, such that we have reduced threats to internal and external validity, making the outcomes more directly applicable to clinical situations. Third, governments around the world and health care systems and policymakers have decided that the quality of care should improve, that it should be evidence based, and that it is in the public's interest to ensure that this happens (Barlow, 2004; Institute of Medicine, 2001).

Of course, the major stumbling block for clinicians everywhere is the accessibility of newly developed evidence-based psychological interventions. Workshops and books can go only so far in acquainting responsible and conscientious practitioners with the latest behavioral health care practices and their applicability to individual patients. This new series, "Treatments That Work™," is devoted to communicating these exciting new interventions to clinicians on the front lines of practice.

The manuals and workbooks in this series contain step-by-step, detailed procedures for assessing and treating specific problems and diagnoses. But this series also goes beyond the books and manuals by providing ancillary materials that will approximate the supervisory process in assisting practitioners in the implementation of these procedures in their practice.

In our emerging health care system, the growing consensus is that evidence-based practice offers the most responsible course of action for the mental health professional. All behavioral health care clinicians deeply desire to provide the best possible care for their patients. In this series, our aim is to close the dissemination and information gap and make that possible.

This therapist guide, and the companion workbook for clients, addresses the treatment of adult attention-deficit/hyperactivity disorder (adult ADHD). This disorder occurs in from 1 percent to 5 percent of adults but is underrecognized and undertreated. With its characteristic symptom picture of hyperactivity, impulsivity, and difficulties focusing attention, adult ADHD can be as impairing as it is in children. Now we have the first evidence-based treatment for adult ADHD from a leading group of clinical investigators at the Massachusetts General Hospital in Boston. After years of research, and with support from the National Institute of Mental Health, this team has developed a treatment that directly attacks the symptoms of ADHD in a collaborative framework with patients. Either as a complement to medication, or for the up to 50 percent of cases where medication is relatively ineffective, every practitioner dealing with this very common presentation will want to add these treatments to their armamentarium.

David H. Barlow, Editor-in-Chief,

Treatments That Work™

Boston, MA

References

Barlow, D. H. (2004). Psychological treatments. *American Psychologist, 59,* 869–878.

Institute of Medicine. (2001). *Crossing the quality chasm: A new health system for the 21st century.* Washington, DC: National Academy Press.

Contents

Introductory Information for Therapists

Background Information and Purpose of This Program

This therapist manual accompanies the client workbook *Mastering Your Adult ADHD*. The treatment and manuals are designed for use by a therapist who is familiar with cognitive-behavioral therapy. The reason we provide both a therapist manual and a client workbook is to help clients with ADHD receive information in two different modalities—verbally from the therapist and in writing in the form of the client workbook. We have found that presenting information in multiple modalities can be helpful for adults with ADHD who have low attention spans. Hence, we recommend that all of the material presented in the client version of the manual also be presented in the treatment sessions, and we recommend that clients have a copy of the client workbook so that they can refer back to it for questions that may come up. You will notice that the chapters in the therapist manual and in the client workbook do not always correspond because additional information is provided in the therapist manual. However, there is a note at the beginning of each session in the therapist manual that indicates which chapter in the client workbook coincides with a given chapter in the therapist manual.

Each of the treatment sessions builds on previous ones. Each session begins with a review of skills learned in previous sessions. Repetition is key to helping adults with ADHD learn skills that they can use long enough for the skills to become easy to implement. If necessary, we recommend spending continued time on skills that have not yet been mastered before moving on to additional skills. The first skills module is on organizing and planning. We consider this module to be the foundation for all additional modules and therefore recommend spending as much time as it takes for clients to learn these skills in order to maximize the chances of the treatment being a success.

ADHD in childhood and adulthood is a valid, reliably diagnosed neurobiological disorder. It can be reliably diagnosed in adults, the diagnosis meets acceptable standards of diagnostic validity, and the functional impairment caused by adult ADHD may include impairment in employment, education, and economic and social functioning (see Biederman et al., 1993, 1996; Murphy & Barkley, 1996a; Spencer et al., 1998). Psychopharmacologic treatment studies (see Wilens et al., 1998a); genetic studies, including adoption (Cantwell, 1972; Morrison & Stewart, 1973; Sprich et al., 2000); and family studies (Biederman et al., 1991, 1992, 1986, 1987; Farone et al., 1991; Goodman, 1989; Goodman & Stevenson, 1989; Morrison, 1980; Lahey et al., 1988; Safer, 1973; Stevenson et al., 1993; Szatmari et al., 1993), as well as neuroimaging and neurochemistry research (e.g., Spencer et al., 2002; Zametkin & Liotta, 1998) and molecular genetic research (see Adler & Chua, 2002) all support that ADHD as a diagnosis meets the guidelines for diagnostic validity standards (i.e., Spitzer & Williams, 1985).

Estimates of the prevalence of ADHD in adulthood range from 1 percent to 5 percent (Bellak & Black, 1992; Biederman et al., 1996; Murphy & Barkley, 1996b). Generally, the symptoms of ADHD in adulthood are similar to those in children, and, although the literature on women and girls is limited, symptoms seem to be similar across both genders (Barkley, 1998; Biederman et al., 1994; 1996). Accordingly, core symptoms in adulthood include impairments in attention, inhibition, and self-regulation. These core symptoms yield associated impairments in adulthood such as poor school and work performance (e.g., trouble with organization and planning, becoming easily bored, deficient sustained attention for reading and paperwork, procrastination, poor time management, impulsive decision making), impaired interpersonal skills (problems with friendships, poor follow-through on commitments, poor listening skills, difficulty with intimate relationships), and other adaptive behavior problems (low level of education for level of ability, poor financial management, trouble organizing one's home, chaotic routine). Our pilot work further details residual symptom presentation in medication-treated adults.

In the following table we list the *DSM-IV* (APA, 1994) criteria for ADHD. Each of the following five criteria (A–E) must be met in order to qualify for a diagnosis of ADHD.

A. **Either six or more of the following symptoms of inattention or six or more of the following symptoms of hyperactivity/impulsivity must be present.**

Symptoms of Inattention	Symptoms of Hyperactivity/Impulsivity
Often fails to give close attention to details or makes careless mistakes in schoolwork, work, or other activities	Often fidgets with hands or feet or squirms in seat
Often has difficulty sustaining attention in tasks or play activities	Often leaves seat in classroom or in other situations in which remaining seated is expected
Often does not seem to listen when spoken to directly	Often runs about or climbs excessively in situations in which it is inappropriate (in adolescents or adults, may be limited to subjective feelings of restlessness)
Often does not follow through on instructions and fails to finish schoolwork, chores, or duties in the workplace (not because of oppositional behavior or failure to understand instructions)	Often has difficulty playing or engaging in leisure activities quietly
Often has difficulty organizing tasks and activities	Is often "on the go" or often acts as if "driven by a motor"
Often avoids, dislikes, or is reluctant to engage in tasks that require sustained mental effort	Often talks excessively
Often loses things necessary for tasks or activities	Often blurts out answers before questions have been completed
Is often easily distracted by extraneous stimuli	Often has difficulty awaiting turn
Is often forgetful in daily activities	Often interrupts or intrudes on others

B. Some symptoms were present before the age of 7.

C. Some impairment from the symptoms is present in two or more settings (e.g., work and home).

D. There must be clear evidence of clinically significant impairment in social, academic, or occupational functioning.

E. The symptoms do not occur exclusively during the course of a pervasive developmental disorder, schizophrenia, or other psychotic disorder and are not better accounted for by another mental disorder (e.g., mood disorder, anxiety disorder, dissociative disorder, or personality disorder).

Distinguishing Between ADHD as a Diagnosis and Normal Functioning

Some of the symptoms listed in the preceding section sound like they might apply to almost anyone at certain times. For example, most people would probably say that they are sometimes easily distracted or sometimes have problems organizing. This is actually the case with many of the psychiatric disorders that exist. For example, everyone gets sad sometimes, but not everyone suffers from a clinical diagnosis of depression.

This is why criteria C and D exist. In order for ADHD to be considered as a medical diagnosis for any individual, he must have significant difficulties with some aspect of his life, such as work, significant relationship problems, and/or significant problems in school.

For ADHD to be considered as an appropriate diagnosis, not only must the distress and impairment be present, but also this distress and impairment must be caused by ADHD and not by another disorder.

Treatment of ADHD with Medications

Medications have been the most extensively studied treatment for adult ADHD. Although medications are highly useful in the treatment of adult ADHD, it appears that they are only partially effective. In controlled studies of stimulant medications, and open studies of tricyclic, monoamine oxidase inhibitor, and atypical antidepressants, 20–50 percent of adults are considered nonresponders due to insufficient symptom reduction or inability to tolerate these medications (Wender, 1998; Wilens et al., 2002a). Moreover, adults who are considered responders typically show a reduction in only 50 percent or fewer of the core symptoms of ADHD, and these response rates are worse than the rates found in children (Wilens et al., 1998a, 2002a). This means that many residual symptoms often persist for adults with ADHD after adequate medication treatment.

Although psychopharmacology may ameliorate many of the core symptoms of ADHD (attentional problems, high activity, impulsivity), it does not provide the client with concrete strategies and skills for coping with associated functional impairment. Quality-of-life impairments such as underachievement, unemployment or underemployment, economic problems, and relationship difficulties associated with ADHD in adulthood (Biederman et al., 1993; Murphy & Barkley, 1996a; Ratey et al., 1992) require active problem-solving, which can be achieved with skills training over and above medication management. Recommendations for the optimal treatment of adult ADHD call for the use of concomitant psychosocial interventions with medications (Biederman et al., 1996; Wender 1998; Wilens et al., 1998 a,b).

Development of This Treatment Program

This program was developed and initially tested at the Cognitive-Behavioral Therapy Program at the Massachusetts General Hospital (Harvard Medical School), Department of Psychiatry. Input for the treatment came from the psychiatrists who run the Adult ADHD program at MGH (Drs. Joseph Biederman, Timothy Wilens, Thomas Spencer) and treat large numbers of adults with ADHD using medications. Through their clinical and research efforts, these providers noticed that medications, although they do help, do not fully treat the problem.

To help conceptualize the treatment, we also reviewed published guidelines about therapy for adult ADHD, including a chart review by Wilens et al. (1999), which reported on a cognitive-behavioral treatment approach developed by Stephen McDermott (McDermott, 2000). This treatment was grounded heavily in cognitive therapy.

Members of our team also met with medication-treated adults with ADHD for their input about the types of problems with which they would want help from a cognitive-behavioral treatment program. The individuals we met with presented problems in (1) organizing and planning, (2) coping with distractibility, (3) managing anxiety and depression, (4) avoiding procrastination. Additional issues included anger and frustration management and communication skills. Examples are discussed below.

Organization and Planning

Problems with organization and planning involve difficulties figuring out the logical, discrete steps to complete tasks that seem overwhelming. For many clients, this difficulty leads to giving up, procrastination, anxiety, and feelings of incompetence and underachievement.

We have had, for example, several clients who were underemployed or unemployed who had never completed thorough job searches. This resulted in their not having a job, working in a much lower-paying position than they could have, or not working at a job that would lead to appropriate employment.

Distractibility

The problems with distractibility involved problems in work or school. Many of our clients have reported that they do not complete tasks because other, less important things get in the way. Examples might include sitting down at one's computer to work on a project but constantly going on the Internet to look up certain Web sites or to browse items on eBay. We had a student in our program who lived alone; whenever he sat down to do his thesis, he would find another place in his apartment to clean (even though it was already basically clean enough).

Mood Problems (Associated Anxiety and Depression)

Secondary to core ADHD symptoms, many of our clients have mood problems. These problems involve worry about events in their lives and sadness regarding either real underachievement or perceived underachievement. Many individuals with ADHD report a strong sense of frustration about tasks that they do not finish or do not do as well as they feel that they could have.

We recently completed a randomized controlled trial of the intervention described in this manual (Safren et al., in press). This study involved comparing the intervention with continued medications to continued medications alone. Thirty-one adults with ADHD and stable psychopharmacology for ADHD were randomized. Assessments included ADHD severity and associated anxiety and depression, rated by an independent evaluator and by self-report. At the outcome assessment, those who were randomized to CBT had significantly lower independent evaluator-rated ADHD symptoms and global severity, as well as self-reported ADHD symptoms, than those randomized to continued psychopharmacology alone. Those in the CBT group also had lower independent evaluator-rated and self-reported anxiety and lower independent evaluator-rated depression, and we also noted a trend toward lower self-reported depression. CBT continued to show superiority over continued psychopharmacology alone when statistically controlling for levels of depression in analyses of core ADHD symptoms. There were significantly more treatment responders among clients who received CBT compared with those who did not. These data support the hypothesis that CBT for adults with ADHD with residual symptoms is a feasible, acceptable, and potentially efficacious next-step treatment approach, worthy of further testing.

In conducting this study, and treating more clients with ADHD following our protocol, we made some refinements to the initial treatment protocol and modules. We found that many participants reported problems specific to organizing papers—and therefore a session has been added on this issue. Also, we added a specific section on family member support because a large proportion of participants requested this assistance.

Currently we are further testing the efficacy of the intervention by comparing it to a second cognitive-behavioral approach—applied relaxation. This is a 5-year study funded by a grant from the National Institute of Mental Health to Dr. Safren.

Although this therapist manual is designed for therapists with some experience with cognitive-behavioral therapy, some important information is presented here. Many of the clients with adult ADHD will not have heard about cognitive-behavioral therapy. A good proportion of clients may have tried other types of therapy, such as supportive therapy or psychodynamic psychotherapy. In order to lay the groundwork for an approach that is likely quite different from previous approaches they have tried (i.e., the sessions have an agenda, the treatment is modular, the treatment requires active homework that is considered to be as important as or more important than what is done in the session itself), we find it important to be able to answer questions about the model behind the treatment approach. Some of this information is also presented in the client workbook.

- **The cognitive component of cognitive-behavioral therapy.** Cognitive components include thoughts and beliefs that can exacerbate ADHD symptoms. For example, a person who is facing something that she will find overwhelming might shift her attention elsewhere or think things like, "I can't do this," "I don't want to do this," or "I will do this later." These thoughts contribute to negative feelings that can interfere with successful completion of the task. Part of this treatment involves restructuring these types of thoughts so that adaptive thinking is maximized.

- **The behavioral component of cognitive-behavioral therapy.** Behavioral components are behaviors, or things people do, that can exacerbate ADHD symptoms. The actual behaviors can include things like avoiding doing what you should be doing or not keeping an organizational system.

Cognitive-Behavioral Model of Adult ADHD

On the following page is an explanation of each of the components of the cognitive-behavioral model.

Core neuropsychiatric impairments, starting in childhood, that prevent effective coping. Adults with ADHD, by definition, have been suffering from this disorder chronically since childhood. Specific symptoms such as distractibility, disorganization, difficulty following through on tasks, and impulsivity can prevent people with ADHD from learning or using effective coping skills.

Lack of effective coping can lead to underachievement and failures. Because of this lack, clients with this disorder typically have sustained underachievement, or have endured experiences that they might label "failures."

Underachievement and failures can lead to negative thoughts and beliefs. This history of failures can result in developing overly negative beliefs about oneself, as well as negative, maladaptive thinking when approaching tasks. The negative thoughts and beliefs that ensue can add to avoidance or distractibility.

Negative thoughts and beliefs can lead to mood problems and can exacerbate avoidance. As a result of such thoughts and beliefs, people shift their attention even more when confronted with tasks or problems, and related behavioral symptoms can also get worse.

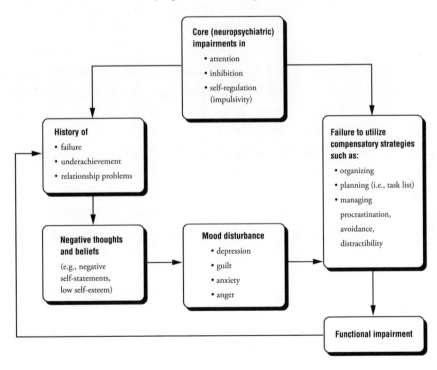

The treatment approach depicted in this manual was designed for and tested on individuals who had already been diagnosed with ADHD and who have been on medications. In our clinical practices, we have found, anecdotally, that delivering the treatment with unmedicated clients or clients who had not taken their medications prior to the session has been somewhat more difficult. Problems with inattention, distractibility, and impulsivity can interfere with the didactic aspects of CBT. Hence, we find it important to inquire about regular medication use and to discuss the importance of adherence to medications, especially in the case of stimulants, which are typically short-acting agents.

Medications are currently the first-line treatment approach for adult ADHD, and they are the most extensively studied. The classes of these medications are stimulants, tricyclic antidepressants, monoamine oxidase inhibitors (antidepressants), and atypical antidepressants. However, a good number of individuals (approximately 20–50 percent) who take antidepressants are considered nonresponders. A nonresponder is an individual whose symptoms are not sufficiently reduced by the medications or who cannot tolerate the medications. Additionally, adults who are considered responders typically show a reduction in only 50 percent or fewer of the core symptoms of ADHD.

Because of these data, recommendations for the best treatment of adult ADHD include using psychotherapy with medications. Medications can reduce many of the core symptoms of ADHD: attentional problems, high activity, and impulsivity. However, medications do not intrinsically provide clients with concrete strategies and skills for coping. Furthermore, disruptions on overall quality of life, such as underachievement, unemployment or underemployment, economic problems, and relationship difficulties associated with ADHD in adulthood call for the application of additional ameliorative interventions.

The treatment involves three core modules: (1) psychoeducation/organizing and planning, (2) reducing distractibility, and (3) adaptive thinking (cognitive restructuring).

Organization and Planning

The first part of the treatment involves organization and planning skills. This includes skills such as:

- Learning to effectively and consistently use a calendar book
- Learning to effectively and consistently use a task list
- Working on effective problem-solving skills, including (1) breaking down tasks into steps and (2) choosing a best solution for a problem when no solution is ideal
- Developing a triage system for mail and papers

Reducing Distractibility

The second part of treatment involves the management of distractibility. Skills include the following:

- Maximizing and building on one's attention span (breaking tasks into steps that correspond to the length of one's attention span, then building on this)
- Using a timer, distractibility reminders, and other techniques (e.g., distractibility delay)

Adaptive Thinking

The third part of treatment involves learning to think about problems and stressors in the most adaptive way possible. This includes

- Positive "self-coaching"

■ Learning how to identify and dispute negative thoughts

■ Learning how to look at situations rationally, and therefore to make rational choices about the best possible solutions

Application to Procrastination

An optional additional module for procrastination exists. We include this because, although most of the previous modules do relate to procrastination, some people require extra help in this area. This module, therefore, specifically points to how to use the learned skills just described to help with procrastination.

Structure of Sessions

The following activities are included in each session.

Setting an agenda. It is important to begin each session by setting an agenda. This helps maintain a structured focus on treatment for ADHD and also prepares the client for what lies ahead in the upcoming session. One of the challenges in this treatment is to avoid getting distracted by discussions of other problems the client may be facing. At times, these problems are pertinent to the client's ADHD difficulties and can be addressed in the context of the session topics. Other times, it is necessary to convey empathy regarding a client's difficulty and to acknowledge that one of the limitations of this treatment is the need to remain focused so all of the skills to manage ADHD symptoms can be reviewed. Inevitably, this means not having time to go into other topics. We recommend assisting clients in identifying other people to whom they can turn for support around other difficulties.

Monitoring of progress. As we have already discussed, this treatment approach involves regularly monitoring improvement. By administering a measure of ADHD symptoms each week, you, as a therapist, can determine whether the skills are helping. Items that do not change on the ADHD assessment can be targets for further discussion. We recommend using the Current Symptoms Scale (Barkley & Murphy,

1998). This symptom rating scale is a widely used adjunctive measure of ADHD (Murphy & Gordon, 1998), includes the *DSM-IV* symptoms, and is undergoing full psychometric evaluation by R. Barkley (NIMH: ADHD in Adults, Comorbidities and Adaptive Impairments). In our outcome study (Safren et al., in press), at baseline, we found its internal reliability to be .85 (coefficient alpha), and it correlated significantly with the blind assessor-rated ADHD severity rating ($r = .56$) and the blind assessor-rated CGI ($r = .45$), both p's < .01. We find it important to start each session with a discussion of the current symptom score, as well as a review of the homework.

Review of homework from the previous week. Each session will also begin with a review of clients' progress implementing skills from each of the previous modules. It is important to acknowledge successes and to problem-solve any difficulties they may be having. Repetition of new skills is critical for individuals with ADHD and will maximize gains made in treatment and increase the likelihood of sustaining improvement. In both the client workbook and the therapist manual, we provide a checklist tool to be used to assess which homework was practiced and where future work is needed.

Additional Discussion Points Regarding the Treatment

Not every topic can be covered at once. Although the treatment approach is modular, clients may have areas of difficulty that will not be addressed until future sessions. The program typically starts with getting a calendar and task list system going. This module also involves learning organizing and planning skills. The next module focuses on distractibility. People sometimes have problems with the first module because they get easily distracted, and techniques for controlling distraction are not covered until the second module. This is something that we discuss in the first module. We present it here because it is a point that can come up in different sessions as the treatment progresses.

The client workbook will aid therapists in delivering this intervention. It is set up in a session-by-session format and, for the most part, corresponds with the sessions in the therapist manual. Therapists will learn, however, that, at times, variability in delivery of the modules is required. In addition, session numbers at times may differ between the two manuals. For example, the family session (Chapter 3 in the client workbook, session 2 in the therapist manual) can take place whenever scheduling is feasible after session 1, ideally at session 2. Depending on when the family session takes places, subsequent session numbers may vary. It is also helpful to note that session 1 in the therapist manual covers material from Chapters 1, 2, and 4 in the client workbook.

We have planned the session content so that an optimal amount of information is presented in each session. We have found that some clients cannot take in a lot of new skills in any one session. We have also found that it is important to leave enough time for problem-solving regarding material from previous sessions, provision of psychosocial support, and "coaching" around the fact that, given the modular framework, not all skills can be learned at once. Finally, limiting the amount of new information in each session allows for practice of relatively few skills per week and allows the therapist to present all of the information even when client distractions emerge.

Module 1
Psychoeducation, Organization, and Planning

Session 1 | *Psychoeducation and Introduction to Organization and Planning Skills*

(Corresponds to Chapters 1, 2, and 4 of the Client Workbook)

Materials Needed

▪ Form: Motivational Exercise: Pros and Cons of Changing

Session Outline

▪ Set agenda

▪ Provide information about ADHD

▪ Determine client's goals for CBT for ADHD

▪ Discuss the structure of the sessions

▪ Explain modular format (some difficult areas will not be addressed until future sessions)

▪ Help client problem-solve potential difficulties with the treatment itself

▪ Review motivational information and exercises

▪ Discuss use of medications to treat ADHD

▪ Introduce the notebook and the calendar book

▪ Discuss involvement of a significant other in treatment

▪ Assign homework

Set Agenda

It is important to begin each session by setting an agenda. This helps maintain a structured focus on treatment for ADHD and also prepares the client for what lies ahead in the upcoming session. One of the challenges in this treatment is to avoid getting distracted by discussions of other problems clients may be facing. At times, these problems are pertinent to the client's ADHD difficulties and can be addressed in the context of the session topics. Other times, it is necessary to convey empathy regarding a client's difficulty and to acknowledge that one of the limitations of this treatment is the need to remain focused so that all of the skills to manage ADHD symptoms can be reviewed. Inevitably, this means not having time to go into other topics. Assist the client in identifying other people to whom they can turn for support around other difficulties.

For this session, the agenda involves providing an overview of the treatment and psychoeducational information about ADHD, doing a motivational exercise, and assigning homework.

Information about ADHD

Although we ask clients to read the first four chapters of the client workbook, a brief discussion of ADHD as a diagnosis is warranted here. This involves a discussion of our view of ADHD in adulthood. Important points to emphasize include:

- That it is a neurobiological disorder
- That it is a valid diagnosis
- That it is not related to anything like laziness or intelligence

The treatment therefore involves actively learning skills. These skills need to be practiced regularly in order for the client to improve. The point is to get a system started and to *stay motivated* to keep it going. It is important to convey the point that people with ADHD do have skills—but the issue is to stay motivated to develop a workable system, and keep using it.

We view this section as a discussion to maximize the fit between the treatment approach and the client's goals. The client workbook lists similar questions and a grid for assisting the client with determining how realistic a goal is. One of the columns in the grid is for "controllability." In determining the goals, it is essential to focus on goals that are controllable. For example, a goal of "getting a new job" depends on many things—including the economy, one's education, and other factors. A more controllable goal would be to do as much as possible to maximize one's chances of getting a new job. This can be operationalized later in the problem-solving section by identifying steps such as updating one's resume, applying for jobs, arranging interviews, and so on.

Questions to Help Client Come Up with Goals

The following questions may be helpful with respect to helping a client come up with her treatment goals.

> *What made you decide to start this treatment now?*
>
> *In what ways would you like to approach tasks differently?*
>
> *What are some issues that others have noticed about how you approach tasks?*
>
> *If you did not have problems with ADHD, what do you think would be different?*

Goal List

Goal of CBT	Controllability (as a percentage)	Short or Long Term

At this point in the session, we provide an overview about the structure of the sessions and provide some information about how to work together with the client so that she gets the most out of treatment. The following list of points should be addressed in this discussion.

- **The therapy will be directive, almost like taking a course.**

  Each session has an agenda, and we will follow specific topics in each session. The topics are also covered in the workbook *Mastering Your Adult ADHD*. We put the information in both places so that clients can easily refer back to the workbook to look up answers to issues that they may forget and so that they can get additional practice. Although all of the sessions' contents are included in the client workbook, we recommend that you discuss the importance of not trying all of the new skills at once with the client.

- **The therapy involves homework.**

  As discussed in the introductory materials, the therapy involves homework. We consider the homework to be as important as, or even more important than, attendance at the sessions. Hence, each session involves a review of the previous week's homework, as well as assignments for the upcoming week. In this way, the treatment is similar to taking a course.

- **The therapy involves regular monitoring of progress.**

  We recommend administering an outcome measure at each session. For adult ADHD, the most widely used measure is the ADHD Current Symptom Scale, which is included in the client workbook. At the beginning of each session, the therapist can review the total score so that progress can be measured and so that the therapist can identify any problem areas that have not been resolved. This can assist in problem-solving any difficulty with homework assignments or skills learned, so that they can be improved on an as-needed basis.

  One point to mention regarding improvement, however, is that sometimes, when clients do cognitive-behavioral therapy, they seem to expect that improvement will be linear. For example, they expect that their symptoms will decrease by 10 percent each week for 10 weeks and then be 100 percent improved. However, this is rarely the case. Typically there are ups and downs along the way—life events occur, skills take time to practice and master. When there is a "down," this is definitely not a time to quit; this is a time to learn from the things that led up to the setback and to figure out how to handle them in the future. This is extremely important with respect to managing expectations. Setbacks that occur in the context of treatment can be viewed as important to treatment planning; they identify areas that can be targeted for additional problem-solving and for the development of coping skills.

- **A potential pitfall with the modular approach is that clients may have areas of difficulty that will not be addressed until future sessions.**

  Discuss any potential problems with the approach and plan how you will address such problems. Emphasize the point that some of these skills may be familiar to the client. However, they work only if they are continually used. Therefore, for certain modules, the goal may be to start or restart using these skills consistently, in order to lay the groundwork for future modules and to lead to more optimal functioning.

- **Practice is highly important.**

  Explain that because ADHD is associated with difficulties with follow-through, some or all of the skills may seem difficult at first. This is the reason for doing the work both with a therapist and by oneself. As a consequence, regular review and practice of skills will occur in the session itself, as well as outside the session during the week. Although these skills may seem difficult at first, with practice they become much easier and eventually become "second nature."

- **Ask about potential problems with the treatment itself.**

  Some difficulties with following the treatment program revolve around attendance, attention, and adherence to the treatment. These problems are part of the diagnosis of ADHD itself but can potentially interfere with the treatment. Convey to the client that when difficulties with follow-through regarding the therapy itself arise, it is important to discuss these difficulties instead of missing a session. Also convey that we realize that difficulties with follow-through can be *part of the disorder itself.* Discuss the importance of attending *all sessions* in order to achieve benefit. Research on most cognitive-behavioral interventions suggests that the more effort a person puts into a treatment, in terms of completing homework and attending sessions, the more the person will benefit.

■ **Discuss a plan for refocusing when the therapist thinks the session may be going off topic.**

One potential difficulty can include staying on topic and sustaining attention. Therefore, the therapist will need to aid in refocusing if and when the topic of importance is no longer being attended to. We discuss this with clients so that they can agree with this plan and not take this refocusing personally. Some potential aids may include:

1. Asking the client to give the therapist permission to utilize a hand signal when its time to refocus.

2. Saying to the client, "This is one of those times where I am now going to interrupt."

3. Discussing ways that the client can communicate the need to take a break.

4. Reminding the client of how much more time is required and what further topics need addressing.

Motivational Information and Exercises

The next section of this session is dedicated to attempting to increase the client's motivation for making changes. Some of these sections can be repeated on an as-needed basis as the treatment continues.

First, we provide an illustration of some of the difficulties involved in doing treatment oriented toward behavior change. This metaphor is one used in Dr. Marsha Linehan's dialectical behavioral therapy treatment program (Linehan, 1993). What follows is some suggested phrasing.

Motivational Metaphor (Optional, Depending on Amount of Time Available in Session)

As we discussed, negative habits can be a cycle. Sometimes negative habits and stress can lead to depressed mood. When you're depressed, it's more difficult to motivate yourself to change, and because you haven't motivated yourself to change, you feel more depressed.

It's kind of like you are stuck in a hole, and the only tool you have is a shovel. You know how to shovel, and it's an easy, comfortable thing to do, but it makes your problem worse—the hole gets deeper. One day, someone comes along and throws down a ladder. The only problem is that the ladder is scalding hot. So if you climb up, it's going to be really difficult and is going to hurt. There won't be permanent damage, but it will be tough to do. If you do it, you will be out of the hole.

Motivational Exercise: Pros and Cons of Changing

1. Introduce the idea of examining the pros and cons of behaviors.

2. Discuss the idea that with ADHD the short-term pros and cons can seem to outweigh the long-term, sometimes more important, pros and cons.

3. Emphasize that the idea is to learn to slow down and evaluate the pros and cons of issues in situations.

4. Complete the sheet on page 29 regarding changing.

5. Emphasize the negative effect of ADHD on client's life.

Discussion Point: Medications

■ Typically ADHD in adulthood is treated with medications. The goal of therapy is to help clients function at their optimal level, utilizing medications and the skills from this therapy to help achieve this goal.

- Discuss the idea that the medications can help a person actually achieve goals of behavioral therapy.

- If not already done, discuss the client's current medications, history with medications, and beliefs about the usefulness of medication.

- Explain that symptoms of ADHD such as distractibility or poor organization may interfere with taking all of a person's prescribed doses or may contribute to difficulty developing a structured routine for taking medication.

- Mention that this treatment will help clients prioritize taking medication and will provide opportunities to work with a therapist and problem-solve around difficulties taking medications. Each week you will discuss factors leading to missed doses.

Notebook and Calendar Systems

Here we introduce the use of the notebook and calendar systems. These provide the essential foundation for systems the client will develop throughout the treatment. It is critical that enough time be spent on this section to ensure that the client understands the rationale for these systems and is ready to create his own system. Stress the importance of having a calendar book for appointments, and explain that the rationale for the notebook is to keep notes on therapy techniques, to record daily and weekly goals by importance, and to record other aspects of this treatment. As part of this discussion, ask the client about past attempts at using organizational systems. Work with the client to problem-solve around any difficulties that were experienced.

Next, try to come up with best organizational system for client to restart using. The organizational system must have a calendar and a notebook. If the client prefers, a Palm Pilot can be used instead. However, we do not recommend that a client begin using a Palm Pilot for the first time during this treatment. The goal is to make the client's system as simple as possible. Having to learn how to use a Palm Pilot can potentially overwhelm the client.

If the client does not already keep a calendar book, this is the principal homework assignment for the next session. Suggest places where the client can purchase a calendar book and a notebook. If necessary, provide the client with a blank notebook to use during treatment. Remind the client that both the notebook and the calendar book should be brought to every session and will be used in most sessions. From this point forward, the client should write ALL appointments in the calendar and should begin a "to-do" list in the notebook. Any task that must be completed should be written in this list. The idea is to eliminate the use of "stickies" or other scraps of paper with notes written on them. All tasks should be written down and managed in one section of the notebook. The client should look at the task list every day to determine which tasks will be completed that day.

Involvement of a Significant Other During Treatment

Over the next several months, the client will be working to develop new skills and habits for managing ADHD. In our experience, having the support and involvement of a family member or significant other can be extremely helpful. It provides an opportunity for the family member to learn more about ADHD and the skills that are taught to help clients manage ADHD. It also enables the client and family member to discuss how AHDH has impacted their relationship. Finally, it enables the client to enlist the support of another person to aid with homework, problem-solve with difficulties in the household related to ADHD, and so on. The next session is optional but is designed to involve a significant other. Discuss the pros and cons of having this optional session, and, if desired, plan the logistics of scheduling a session with a significant other.

Potential Pitfalls

Clients may be reluctant to make significant changes that will decrease the impact of ADHD on their lives. They may feel overwhelmed, pessimistic about their success, or worried about having time to practice skills at home. It can be helpful to emphasize that you will be guiding them to make changes gradually and that you will work together to make the new skills feel manageable. It is certainly inevitable that new behaviors will feel different, perhaps uncomfortable, at first and may not lead to success immediately. Sometimes thinking about change in terms of an experiment can be helpful. We suggest encouraging clients to try new strategies for several months to give them a real chance of becoming more familiar and automatic. In the end, clients can always go back to their old ways, but we fully believe that they will have success with this treatment.

Homework

- Purchase a calendar and notebook.
- Write all appointments in the calendar and start ONE master "to-do" list in the notebook.
- Read over the materials for the next session.
- If agreed upon, the client should discuss having a family member attend the next session and contact the therapist to arrange scheduling if necessary.

Case Vignette

T: I've now given you an overview of CBT for ADHD. Can you imagine any difficulties you may have with the treatment?

C: Well, in theory it all sounds good, but I just don't see how it will help me. I've tried all those self-help books, and they never work.

T: Why do you think they don't work?

C: I can stick with it for a week or two, and then I just go back to my old ways.

T: That is a really good point. For most people, change is hard, and change takes time. With ADHD, it can be especially difficult to stay motivated long enough to let the skills sink in and really work. This treatment was designed with that in mind. You will not be alone in this! I will be working very closely with you to help you stay motivated. In addition, we have broken all the skills down into very manageable sections, so you will learn one piece at a time. What we have also found to be helpful is that you and I will review these skills over and over, so it will really help them become more familiar. In the end, it won't take as much effort; these skills will be automatic. I really think you can do it. I'll be working with you if you run into any problems; we'll put our heads together to figure out how to get around your difficulties.

C: I guess I can give it a shot. I know nothing will get better unless I try something new.

T: Exactly! I really believe you will benefit from this treatment. It gets easier as you go along.

Motivational Exercise: Pros and Cons of Changing

New Strategy to Be Considered

	PRO	CON
Short-term consequences		
Long-term consequences		

New Strategy to Be Considered

	PRO	CON
Short-term consequences		
Long-term consequences		

Session 2 | *Involvement of Family Member (if Applicable)*

(Corresponds to Chapter 3 of the Client Workbook)

Materials Needed

- ADHD Symptom Severity Scale
- Form: Client Responses
- Form: Family Member Responses

Session Outline

- Set agenda
- Review Symptom Severity Scale
- Review medication adherence
- Provide education about ADHD from Chapter 1
- Provide overview of the CBT model of the continuation of ADHD into adulthood
- Discuss ways in which ADHD has affected client's relationship with a family member
- Solicit feedback from the family member on the client's symptom severity
- Discuss the family member's role during client's treatment

Set Agenda

It is important to begin each session by setting an agenda. Review the session outline with the client and family member. It may be helpful to review the rationale for agenda setting for the family member. Explain that you will be setting an agenda so that everyone will know what to expect in the session and to ensure that you remain focused on helping the client and family member learn more about managing ADHD. You will also address ways in which ADHD may impact the relationship. It is helpful to acknowledge that you probably won't be able to cover everything in this one session, but you will try to make the best use of this time.

Review of Symptom Severity Scale

Per usual, the client completes the ADHD self-report symptom checklist at the beginning of the session. Briefly review the score, and take note of symptoms that have improved and those that are still problematic. You can also have the significant other complete a checklist about the client's symptoms. As therapy progresses, it can be helpful to continue to get collateral information about the patient's improvement by asking the significant other to complete these on a regular basis.

Score: _____

Date: _____

Review of Medication Adherence

Each week the client records her prescribed dosage of medication and indicates the number of doses that were missed during the week. Assist the client in identifying triggers for missed doses, such as distractibility, running out of medication, or thoughts about not wanting/needing to take medication. Problem-solve as necessary to increase adherence.

Prescribed doses per week: _____

Doses missed this week: _____

Triggers for missed doses: _____

_____

_____

Review of Material From Chapter 1

The goal of this session is to provide the family member with the educational information that was presented in the previous chapter. Realistically, there will not be enough time to cover the material in its entirety. Review the sections that dispel myths about ADHD, and introduce the cognitive-behavioral model of ADHD. Finally, discuss some of the techniques that will be utilized during treatment, such as the notebook and calendar system. In addition, it is important to discuss the role of homework completion in the client's success with the treatment. This may be a critical area in which the family member may be able to provide encouragement throughout the program.

Discuss How ADHD Has Affected the Relationship

ADHD can certainly contribute to strained relationships with family members, especially when they are not familiar with the symptoms of ADHD and associated difficulties. We provide two worksheets to assist the client and family member in this discussion. Instruct each to complete their respective worksheet separately, and then discuss their responses. You may not have time to review all of the questions in the session. Help initiate this process, and assign a continued discussion for homework.

It is important to keep in mind that there may be other relationship difficulties that create tension. Your role is not to conduct couples therapy, and you will not have time to go into these issues in depth! It can be helpful to acknowledge that there are other important areas for the family members to work on and to suggest alternative resources. Try to maintain a focus on how the client's ADHD affects the relationship and how the family members can work together to problem-solve in this area.

Discuss the Family Member's Role During Treatment

Having the support of a family member can enhance the client's success in cognitive-behavioral therapy. Family members can remind clients to complete homework each day, can assist in identifying locations for storing important items (from the Distractibility section), and can provide general support and encouragement. It is important that both family members agree on acceptable ways of providing support. For example, it may not be effective for a family member to nag the client multiple times a day about homework. However, the client may feel that a gentle daily reminder would be helpful.

Discuss How ADHD Has Affected the Relationship

Use the following forms, completed by the client and family member, to begin a discussion about how ADHD has affected the relationship.

Client Responses

What are the symptoms of ADHD that you think are most problematic for you?

_____

_____

_____

_____

_____

What are the three most important ways that these symptoms have affected your relationship with _____ ?

1. _____

_____

_____

2. _____

_____

_____

3. _____

_____

_____

Family Member Responses

Which symptoms of ADHD do you think are most problematic for your family member?

_____

_____

_____

_____

_____

What are the three most important ways that these symptoms have affected your relationship with _____ ?

1. _____

_____

_____

2. _____

_____

_____

3. _____

_____

_____

To enlist the support of the spouse, and to continue to instill credibility and confidence in the treatment, it can be useful to preview the treatment modules and to discuss with the spouse how she can relate to the effect of ADHD on the relationship. Explain about each module and brainstorm ways that spouses can help.

1. **Organization and planning.** The central goal of this first set of sessions is to develop a comprehensive system for organizing and planning. This means consistently using a calendar and task list system (looking at the task list and calendar daily), learning problem-solving skills, and managing organization. Areas in which the significant other can help can include:

    ▪ Ensuring that important events that they will participate in together are entered in the calendar book

    ▪ Assisting with prioritization of tasks, and, if a mutually agreed-on important task arises, making sure that it gets included on the task list

    ▪ Helping the client find a place for important items (keys, wallet, cell phone) and, if these items are seen in another place, moving them back to the designated place

    ▪ Providing positive feedback

2. **Reducing distractibility.** The central goal of this set of sessions is to learn tools for reducing distractibility. This entails learning about the length of one's attention span and breaking tasks into steps that take that amount of time. It also involves skills like "distractibility delay" and modifying one's environment to so that work can be done efficiently.

3. **Adaptive thinking.** The central goal of this module is to learn to think more adaptively (or positively) about situations or tasks. This involves learning to identify one's thoughts, look at the relationship between thoughts and mood, identify evidence for or against the thought, and then come up with an alternate way of thinking about things.

Current Symptoms Self-Report Form

Week of:

Instructions: Please check the response next to each item that best describes your behavior *during the past week.*

		Never or Rarely	Sometimes	Often	Very Often
1	Fail to give close attention to details or make careless mistakes in my work				
2	Fidget with hands or feet or squirm in seat				
3	Have difficulty sustaining my attention in tasks or fun activities				
4	Leave my seat in situations in which seating is expected				
5	Don't listen when spoken to directly				
6	Feel restless				
7	Don't follow through on instructions and fail to finish work				
8	Have difficulty engaging in leisure activities or doing fun things quietly				
9	Have difficulty organizing tasks and activities				
10	Feel "on the go" or "driven by a motor"				
11	Avoid, dislike, or am reluctant to engage in work that requires sustained mental effort				
12	Talk excessively				
13	Lose things necessary for tasks or activities				
14	Blurt out answers before questions have been completed				
15	Am easily distracted				
16	Have difficulty awaiting turn				
17	Am forgetful in daily activities				
18	Interrupt or intrude on others				

From R. A. Barkley & K. R. Murphy (1998), *Attention-Deficit Hyperactivity Disorder: A clinical workbook* (2nd ed.). New York: Guilford Press.

Current Symptoms Family Member Report Form

Instructions: Please check the response next to each item that best describes your family member's behavior *during the past week.*

		Never or Rarely	Sometimes	Often	Very Often
1	Fails to give close attention to details or makes careless mistakes in work				
2	Fidgets with hands or feet or squirms in seat				
3	Has difficulty sustaining attention in tasks or fun activities				
4	Leaves seat in situations in which seating is expected				
5	Doesn't listen when spoken to directly				
6	Feels restless				
7	Doesn't follow through on instructions and fails to finish work				
8	Has difficulty engaging in leisure activities or doing fun things quietly				
9	Has difficulty organizing tasks and activities				
10	Feels "on the go" or "driven by a motor"				
11	Avoids, dislikes, or is reluctant to engage in work that requires sustained mental effort				
12	Talks excessively				
13	Loses things necessary for tasks or activities				
14	Blurts out answers before questions have been completed				
15	Is easily distracted				
16	Has difficulty awaiting turn				
17	Is forgetful in daily activities				
18	Interrupts or intrudes on others				

Adapted from R. A. Barkley & K. R. Murphy (1998), *Attention-Deficit Hyperactivity Disorder: A clinical workbook* (2nd ed.). New York: Guilford Press.

Potential Pitfalls

A common concern among therapists is that the client will feel victimized and attacked when problematic symptoms are identified. The therapist sets the stage for a constructive session by acknowledging that ADHD does not mean that a person is lazy or weak. Rather, it requires that the client use skills and strategies to cope with symptoms effectively. To that end, this session is an opportunity for family members to receive education about ADHD and cognitive-behavioral therapy and for the family members to collaborate with each other and identify strategies for providing support for the client during treatment.

Homework

- The client and family member should continue the discussion on how ADHD has affected their relationship.

- They should continue to discuss ways in which the family member can provide support while the client is in treatment.

- The client should read over the materials for the next session.

Case Vignette

T: We have now reviewed the educational materials on ADHD and discussed the outline of CBT treatment. Let's spend some time thinking about how FM can support you during treatment. C, what kind of support do you think will be most helpful for you?

C: I think finding time to do homework. There are so many demands between my job, our family, and taking care of the house. I'm lucky if I can get those tasks done.

FM: Maybe we can think of a task that I could do for you so that you would have a little more time to work on CBT skills at home.

T: That is a great idea! We don't want you to feel too burdened, but if there is one task you could be responsible for during this 12-week treatment, that would be helpful. C, what do you think?

C: I feel badly that she'd be doing more work than she already does. I guess I would want to make sure she was really okay doing that.

FM: You can trust me on this, but if there are days when I need some extra help, I promise I will let you know.

T: So what would be the task to hand over?

C: I think the best time for me to do homework is first thing in the morning. If she could get breakfast together, it would give me 15 minutes to work on homework. Would that be okay?

FM: I could definitely try that out.

T: I think what you'll find is that if C takes those 15 minutes in the morning, he will actually be more organized and productive during the day, which will help out FM as well in the end.

C: That's true.

FM: Yes.

T: This is a great start! Keep in mind that you can revise your strategies. Sit down in a few weeks, and check in with each other to see how things are going. Ask if either one of you feels more burdened. With communication, these challenges can be addressed. Good luck!

Session 3 | *Organization of Multiple Tasks*

(Corresponds to Chapters 4 and 5 of the Client Workbook)

Materials Needed

- Symptom Severity Scale

Session Outline

- Set agenda
- Review the symptom severity scale
- Review medication adherence
- Review client's use of the calendar and task list
- Teach client how to manage multiple tasks
- Teach client how to prioritize tasks
- Problem-solve regarding any anticipated difficulties using this technique
- Assign homework

Set Agenda

It is important to begin each session by setting an agenda. Review the session outline with the client.

Review of Symptom Severity Scale

Per usual, the client completes the ADHD self-report symptom checklist at the beginning of the session. Briefly review the score, and take note of symptoms that have improved and those that are still problematic.

Score: _____

Date: _____

Review of Medication Adherence

Each week the client records his prescribed dosage of medication and indicates the number of doses that were missed during the week. Assist the client in identifying triggers for missed doses, such as distractibility, running out of medication, or thoughts about not wanting/needing to take medication. Problem-solve as necessary to increase adherence.

Prescribed doses per week: _____

Doses missed this week: _____

Triggers for missed doses: _____

_____

_____

Review of Previous Modules

Review the client's progress implementing skills from each of the previous modules. It is important to acknowledge the successes the client has achieved and to problem-solve around any difficulties.

Review: Tools for Organization and Planning

- Calendar for managing appointments: At this point, you should discuss any problems that the client is having with using his calendar system.

- Notebook for recording a to-do list: Review any difficulties that the client is having with writing down and using his to-do list on a daily basis.

Remind the client that having a good calendar and task list system is necessary (but not sufficient) to getting organized.

If the client has not yet purchased a notebook or calendar book, problem-solving should be conducted around this issue as the client cannot effectively proceed with the treatment until these items have been obtained.

If the client has obtained a notebook or calendar book, review specifics with the client:

- Where will the book be kept?

- How will the client remember to use it every day?

- How will the client remember to look at the task list every day? (The client should pick a time or activity that already occurs every day to link with looking at the task list, such as feeding the dog, having her morning coffee, or brushing her teeth.) The importance of looking at the list every day should be stressed.

Managing Multiple Tasks

We often need to manage multiple tasks at one time. Individuals with ADHD can find it extremely difficult to decide which task is most important. Even once they have decided that a particular task is important, it is often difficult for them to stick with it until it is completed. Other less important tasks can become distractions (i.e., cleaning, making phone calls), and the critical task gets overlooked.

The following exercise teaches clients a concrete strategy to decide which tasks are most important. This technique is one example of how individuals can "force themselves" to organize tasks, even though it is difficult for people with ADHD to process this type of information.

When clients are faced with a number of tasks that must be completed, it is important to have a clear strategy for prioritizing which tasks are most important so that the most important tasks get completed. A useful strategy is to develop a system for assigning a priority rating to each task.

Talk with client about the fact that people often like to complete the tasks that are easier but less important first. This gives the impression of getting things accomplished, but one never makes progress toward important goals. So it *seems* to work in the short-term but actually does not work in the long-term. By adding "A," "B," and "C" ratings to the task list, clients can address this issue. Instruct clients that it works best to list all of the tasks first, and then assign the priority ratings.

"A" Tasks: These are the tasks of highest importance. This means that they must be completed in the short term (like today or tomorrow).

"B" Tasks: These are tasks of less importance, to be done over the long term. Some portions of the task should be completed in the short term, but the other portions may take longer.

"C" Tasks: Lowest importance tasks that may be more attractive and easier to do but are not as important as tasks with higher rankings.

A goal of this session is to help the client generate a task list and then assign a rating of "A," "B," or "C" to each item. Attention should be paid to how many items are being assigned to each category. Clients may tend to assign all items an "A" rating, thus making the strategy less useful.

Talk with client about making sure that all "A" items are completed before moving on to the "B" items and making sure that all "B" items are completed before moving on to the "C" items. Emphasize the importance of sticking to this rule in order for the strategy to be effective. Tell the client to use this technique every day. He should copy over the to-do list when the old one becomes too messy.

Use the sample form to demonstrate what a to-do list should look like.

Task List

Priority Rating	Task	Date Put on List	Date Completed
A			
·			
·			
·			
·			
·			
·			
B			
·			
·			
·			
·			
·			
·			
C			
·			
·			
·			
·			
·			
·			

Potential Pitfalls

The client may become discouraged or feel overwhelmed when trying to learn these new strategies. Encourage the client to stick with the strategy until it becomes more comfortable. Talk with the client about the fact that it takes time to change longstanding habits, and review the benefits of becoming more organized and more effective at completing long-term goals. Problem-solve with the client about any specific difficulties that she may be encountering.

Homework

- Write all appointments in the calendar and use the notebook every day to record and review the to-do list.

- Use and look at task list and calendar EVERY DAY!

- Rate each task as an "A," "B," or "C" task.

- Practice doing all of the "A" tasks before the "B" tasks and all of the "B" tasks before the "C" tasks.

- Carry over tasks that are not completed, and cross out the ones that are.

Case Vignette

T: Let's take a look at your to-do list.

C: Okay.

T: I see that you have three things on your list for today. Let's figure out if each item should be rated as an "A," "B," or "C" task.

C: This is going to be difficult.

T: Well, let's just take one item at a time. The first one is "clean out the cat's litter box." What rating should we give that one?

C: Well, it's pretty messy and it smells bad. I think my kids will really start to complain if that doesn't get done today.

T: Okay. Let's assign that an "A" rating. How about the next one, "call hair salon for appointment"?

C: Well, I do need a hair appointment sometime soon, but I guess it wouldn't be the end of the world if I waited a few days on that one. It would only take a few minutes to do it, though, and then I could cross it off my list.

T: I think that we should probably make that one a "C." It is the type of attractive task that people often want to complete because it is easy and straightforward. The problem is that you can get so busy with these small tasks that the more important ones never get completed. How about if you complete this one after you have completed the more important "A" and "B" tasks?

C: Sure. That makes sense.

T: The third item is "update resume." What rating should we give that one?

C: Well, I have been out of work for a couple of months and money is really getting tight. I should really do that soon. I just get overwhelmed whenever I think about working on my resume.

T: It sounds like an important task, but maybe it is too large to tackle all at once. Can you think of a way to break off a smaller piece of the task?

C: How about printing out my resume and proofreading it?

T: Okay. Let's rewrite this as "print out resume and proofread" and rate that one as an "A."

C: Sounds good.

Session 4 | *Problem-Solving and Managing Overwhelming Tasks*

(Corresponds to Chapter 6 of the Client Workbook)

Materials Needed

- ADHD Symptom Severity Scale
- Problem-Solving Form: Selection of an Action Plan

Session Outline

- Set agenda
- Review symptom severity scale
- Review medication adherence
- Review client's use of the calendar and task list and A, B, C priority ratings
- Teach the client to use problem-solving to overcome difficulties with task completion or selection of a solution to a problem
- Teach client how to break a large task down into small, manageable steps
- Problem-solve regarding any anticipated difficulties using this technique
- Assign homework

Set Agenda

It is important to begin each session by setting an agenda. Review the session outline with the client.

Review of Symptom Severity Scale

Per usual, the client completes the ADHD self-report symptom check-list at the beginning of the session. Briefly review the score and discuss symptoms that have improved or are still problematic.

Score: _____

Date: _____

Review of Medication Adherence

Each week, the client records her prescribed dosage of medication and indicates the number of doses that were missed during the week. Assist the client in identifying triggers for missed doses, such as distractibility, running out of medication, or thoughts about not wanting/needing to take medication. Problem-solve as necessary to increase adherence.

Prescribed doses per week: _____

Doses missed this week: _____

Triggers for missed doses: _____

_____

_____

Review of Previous Modules

Review the client's progress implementing skills from each of the previous modules. It is important to acknowledge the successes the client has achieved and to problem-solve around any difficulties.

It is critical that the client start implementing the use of the calendar book and task list. One potential pitfall with this is that individuals with ADHD may postpone purchasing a calendar/task list system because they are searching for the perfect system. Using a calendar and task list, however, is critical for all of the sessions to come, and it is important to encourage the client to just make a decision and pick one, despite the fact that it may not be the cheapest option, the very best option, and so on.

Review: Tools for Organization and Planning

- Calendar for managing appointments
- Notebook for recording a to-do list
- Use of the "A," "B," and "C" priority ratings

Problem-Solving Strategies

This section involves helping the client learn to recognize when he she is having difficulty completing a task or is becoming overwhelmed and cannot figure out exactly where to start. Explain that this situation can lead to procrastination and other problems.

These problem-solving strategies can help in such situations.

Two key skills will be taught:

1. Selecting an action plan

2. Breaking down an overwhelming task into manageable steps.

The Problem-Solving form will be used to select an action plan.

Explain that developing an action plan can be helpful when it is difficult to determine how to resolve a problem or when the possibility of numerous solutions becomes overwhelming. Selecting an action plan involves the five steps in problem-solving that are listed here.

Use these instructions in conjunction with the form on the following page.

1.   **Articulate the problem.**

Try to get the client to describe the problem in as few words as possible—one to two sentences at the most. Examples might be "I cannot decide whether I should quit my job" and "I cannot decide what to do about a coworker who I can't stand."

2.   **List all possible solutions.**

In these columns the client should try to come up with a number of solutions, regardless of how possible they are, what the consequences may be, or whether or not they sound outrageous. The idea is to really generate a list of as many solutions as possible.

3.   **List the pros and cons of each solution.**

Now is the time for the client to realistically appraise each solution. In these columns the client should figure out what she really thinks would happen if she were to select that solution. The pros (advantages) and cons (disadvantages) of each should be listed.

4.   **Rate each solution.**

In the final column, the client should rate the pros and cons of the solution on a scale from 1 to 10. This should be done as objectively as possible.

5.   **Implement the best option.**

Now that the client has rated each option on a scale of 1 to 10, each rating should be reviewed. Look at the one that is rated the highest. Determine if this is really the solution that the client would like to pick. If so, help the client use the other skills he has learned in this treatment program (problem-solving, organizing, to-do list, calendar book) to implement it.

Problem-Solving Form: Selection of an Action Plan

Statement of the problem: _____

_____

_____

Instructions for form:
1. List all of the possible solutions that you can think of. List them even if you think they don't make sense or you don't think you would do them. The point is to come up with AS MANY solutions AS POSSIBLE.
2. List the pros and cons of each solution.
3. After listing the pros and cons of each, give a rating, review the whole list, and give a rating to each solution.
4. Use additional copies of this form as needed (even if it's for the same problem).

Possible Solution	Pros of Solution	Cons of Solution	Overall Rating of Solution (1–10)

Explain to the client that by learning how to break large tasks down into smaller, more manageable, steps, she will increase the likelihood of starting (and therefore eventually completing) important tasks.

Steps for Breaking Large Tasks Down into Manageable Steps

1. Choose a difficult or complex task from the to-do list (or the "solution plan" from the previous exercise).

2. List the steps that must be completed.

    This can be done using small note cards or plain paper. Ask questions such as "What is the first thing that you would need to do to make this happen?" or "What is next?"

3. For each step, make sure that it is manageable.

    Have the client ask herself, "Is this something that you could realistically complete in one day?" and "Is this something that I would want to put off doing?" If the step itself is overwhelming, then that step should be broken up into steps.

4. List each individual step on the daily to-do list.

Potential Pitfalls

Clients may find that their distractibility interferes with their ability to use these skills. Reassure the client that he will be learning additional skills to deal with distractibility in future sessions. Emphasize the importance of focusing on one set of skills at a time in order to make progress.

Also, clients may report difficulty with rating the pros, cons, and overall desirability of solutions. Again, it should be reiterated that this is a new skill and will take lots of practice before it feels completely comfortable for them.

Again, a big potential pitfall has to do with implementing a calendar and task list system. If, by now, the client has not been able to purchase or find a good system, he should be encouraged to get one immediately after the session (and/or postpone the next session's agenda and walk over to the store with the client as part of the session and help the client pick one out).

Homework

- Continue to write all appointments in the calendar.
- Use notebook every day to review the to-do list.
- Use and look at task list and calendar EVERY DAY!
- Rate each task as an "A," "B," or "C" task.
- Practice doing all of the "A" tasks before the "B" tasks and all of the "B" tasks before the "C" tasks.
- Carry over tasks that are not completed to the next day's to-do list.
- Practice using the problem-solving worksheet for at least one item on the to-do list.
- Practice breaking down one large task from the to-do list into smaller steps.

Case Vignette

T: Let's look at your to-do list and see if there is anything that needs to be broken down into smaller steps.

C: Okay. How about this one: "organize wife's surprise birthday party"?

T: That sounds like a good one. What are the steps that you need to take to do that?

C: I need to decide where I want to have it.

T: What would some other steps be?

C: I need to call and make sure that the place is available on the day I need and make a reservation.

T: Sounds good. Then what do you need to do?

C: I need to make up a guest list.

T: How are you going to let the guests know about the party?

C: I was thinking of sending out invitations. I guess I need to make or buy the invitations, buy some stamps, write out the invitations, and then send them out.

T: Put each of those steps down as separate items on your list. Can you think of any other things that you need to do?

C: I need to speak with the restaurant about the menu, buy some decorations, order a cake, and buy my wife a present.

T: You can put each of those down on your list, as well.

C: Now I have a long list of things to do. What do I do next?

T: You can take that list and then move things onto your daily to-do list. So, what do you want to do from that list tomorrow?

C: I guess I should start by deciding where I want to have the party and making a reservation.

T: Okay, so put those two things down on tomorrow's to-do list. What do you want to do the following day?

C: I could make up the guest list and buy invitations.

T: Sounds good. Do you think you can finish this process for homework?

C: Yes. I feel much better now. Instead of having this huge task hanging over my head that is overwhelming, I can see how I might actually be able to complete it by doing a couple of small things each day.

Session 5 | *Organizing Papers*

(Corresponds to Chapter 7 of the Client Workbook)

Materials Needed

- Symptom Severity Scale
- Form: Steps for Sorting Mail
- Form: Developing a Filing System

Session Outline

- Set agenda
- Review symptom severity scale
- Review medication adherence
- Review client's use of the calendar, task list and A, B, C priority ratings, problem-solving, and breaking down large tasks into small steps
- Teach client to develop a sorting system for mail
- Teach client how to develop a filing system for papers
- Problem-solve regarding any anticipated difficulties using this technique
- Assign homework

Set Agenda

It is important to begin each session by setting an agenda. Review the session outline with the client.

Review of Symptom Severity Scale

Per usual, the client completes the ADHD self-report symptom checklist at the beginning of the session. Briefly review the score and take note of symptoms that have improved and those that are still problematic.

Score: _____

Date: _____

Review of Medication Adherence

Each week the client records his prescribed dosage of medication and indicates the number of doses that were missed during the week. Assist the client in identifying triggers for missed doses, such as distractibility, running out of medication, or thoughts about not wanting/needing to take medication. Problem-solve as necessary to increase adherence.

Prescribed doses per week: _____

Doses missed this week: _____

Triggers for missed doses: _____

_____

_____

Review of Previous Modules

Review the client's progress implementing skills from each of the previous modules. It is important to acknowledge the successes the client has achieved and to problem-solve around any difficulties.

Review: Tools for Organization and Planning

■ Calendar for managing appointments

■ Notebook for recording a to-do list

- Use of the "A," "B," and "C" priority ratings

- Use of problem-solving (selecting an action plan and breaking down large tasks into small steps).

Skill: Developing a Sorting System for Mail

Most people find it somewhat difficult to organize mail, important papers, and bills. However, people with ADHD can find it overwhelming. This can lead to arguments with roommates or family members, failure to pay bills on time, and the misplacing of important documents. This can be extremely frustrating and upsetting for the client, as well as for the client's family members and friends.

Explain to the client that putting a structured system in place can make this issue feel less overwhelming and more manageable. Discuss how the process may be difficult in the short term, but, in the long-term, it will make things much easier. Be sure to specify the benefits of having an organizational system in the long term (decreased feelings of being overwhelmed, fewer late fees, not missing out on opportunities due to lost paperwork or missed deadlines).

We recommend involving the client's spouse, partner, or roommate to develop a system that is mutually agreeable.

Use the Steps for Sorting Mail form to help the client develop a system for her mail. As part of this process, talk with the client about her current strategy for paying bills. One common concern of individuals with ADHD is that they don't want to pay the bill until that last minute. Some people feel that this will save money as they won't lose out on the interest that their money earns in the bank. Other people feel that they want to wait because they want to have their money longer. Others just simply procrastinate paying bills. Typically, what happens is that people who try this end up paying bills late, incurring fees, and actually losing money. Suggest that it might actually be a more effective strategy for the client to deal with bills and other household to-do items right away. We suggest that clients use the triage system three times a week and deal with each piece of mail at that time. Talk about the benefits of the OHIO (Only Handle It Once) technique with the client.

1. Identify a central location for your triage center: This is where all incoming mail, bills, and paperwork will be opened and sorted. You can use a wicker basket, file tray, drawer, bowl, or box for this purpose.

   Central location for you _____

2. Figure out "rules" regarding keeping mail, bills, and paperwork (e.g., I will save all bills for 6 months, I will pay bills right away).

3. Gather all necessary items to keep with triage center. Keep your checkbook, stamps, pens, calculator, address book, and other supplies nearby so that it is not necessary to go searching for these items when you need to pay a bill or respond to a letter.

4. Identify two or three times per week to go through the items in the triage center and take any action that is required (pay bill, make phone call, respond to letter). Use your calendar book and task list to help with planning this.

5. Write your "triage times" in your calendar. Problem-solve to make sure that you are not choosing times when it is unrealistic to think that you will have enough time to deal with all of the items or when you will be too tired or stressed to be effective at this task.

6. If you experience negative thoughts and you want to give up, try not to give in to this impulse. You will learn how to cope with negative thoughts in the upcoming module on adaptive thinking.

Another common struggle for people with ADHD is keeping papers organized. Without a system in place, papers easily get lost, leading to frustration when they are needed again, or deadlines are missed because important information cannot be found. Furthermore, many people find it difficult to throw away papers, resulting in so much clutter that it becomes even harder to manage the important papers. We recommend a system that is both simple and effective. Some people try to have a complicated system of filing, with many subfiles, subfolders, and so on. This becomes difficult to use and takes too much time to use, and people therefore stop using it.

Ask the client about systems she has used in the past or is currently using. Instruct the client that the filing system should be used for THE MOST IMPORTANT ITEMS ONLY. We recommend that anything that the client does not critically need should be thrown away. The client's spouse or partner can help to develop the decision rules for this. Many individuals with ADHD tend to "hoard" items, thinking that they may be needed later. Review the guidelines in the handout to help the client develop a system or improve upon one that is already in place.

1. Decide where you will keep your filing system. *(Don't spend too much time making this decision.)*

2. Pick one or two file drawers or a small filing cabinet to use. Keep it simple! You need to keep only things that you will *really* need.

3. Buy hanging file folders for main categories and smaller folders for subcategories.

4. Set up your main files (automobile, medical information, taxes, bank statements, credit card statements).

5. Set up your subcategories (e.g., in credit card file, you could have subfiles for Mastercard, Visa, American Express, and so on). Try to keep the system simple. As the system becomes more complicated, the likelihood that you will use it is reduced.

6. Plan specific times each week that you will use the filing system. Problem-solve to make sure that you are not choosing unrealistic times.

7. Remember that it is important to practice these skills for long enough that they become a habit. Don't give up too soon!

Clients may think that everything is important. Ask the client to discuss this issue with friends and family and to come up with a firm list.

Encourage the client to invest the time in the short term to set up these systems. Talk about the value of having these systems in place in the long term. Coach the client regarding breaking down the steps of setting up the systems into smaller steps.

Talk with the client about the utility of discussing the triage and filing systems with other family members before setting them up. Discuss possible issues with the systems if this step is skipped (if the spouse is still putting the mail in a big pile on the chair and the client is trying to use the triage system, it won't work very well).

Homework

- Continue to use the calendar and notebook every day to record appointments and review the to-do list.

- Use and look at task list and calendar EVERY DAY!

- Rate each task as an "A," "B," or "C" task.

- Practice doing all of the "A" tasks before the "B" tasks and all of the "B" tasks before the "C" tasks.

- Carry over tasks that are not completed to the next day's to-do list.

- Practice using the problem-solving worksheet for at least one item on the to-do list.

- Practice breaking down one large task from the to-do list into smaller steps.

- Set up and use the triage and filing systems developed in session.

T: What do you think you could use as your triage center for sorting mail?

C: I could use a wire basket that I have on my desk. Right now it is filled with a random assortment of papers, but if I cleaned it out, I could use it as a place to put all of my mail that needs to be sorted.

T: That sounds good. What will your rules be for sorting your mail?

C: I always feel like I need to keep things just in case I might need them in the future, but I guess that's not always helpful.

T: So what might be a more effective rule?

C: Well, I could ask myself what is the worst thing that would happen if I didn't save it.

T: How would that translate into a rule?

C: I could say that if I can't think of a reason why I am definitely going to need the paper or anything terrible that will happen if I don't save it, I will throw it away.

T: Okay, though I have a feeling that you will still find everything to be important.

C: No, that's not true.

T: Well, let's think of an example. Let's say you get an invitation to go to an event and you want to go.

C: I would need to keep that.

T: Well, I am just wondering. Is that the kind of thing that you could centralize—I mean write down the important information, like the location, the time, and a phone number, in your calendar book and thus eliminate the need for an additional piece of paper that you would need to keep track of.

C: Well, that would be totally radical!

T: This is the kind of thing I am talking about—the big, difficult goal of really trying to reduce as much paper as possible, and really trying to centralize EVERYTHING in your calendar and task list.

C: Uhm, okay. Well, I guess I could try that out.

T: Okay, so what other things do you want to keep near your triage center?

C: I think I should keep stamps, envelopes, pens, scissors, and my checkbook and calculator.

T: Is there anything else that you might need?

C: Maybe my address book. There are a couple of bills that I need to pay, like my office rent, that I don't get statements for and I just need to send them to the right address.

T: What times do you want to choose to use your triage center? Remember, you should choose times when you can actually deal with the bills, phone calls, and so on.

C: I think I could do it before work on Monday, Wednesday, and Friday.

T: Do you have enough time then?

C: I think so. I have about an hour free between the time that the kids leave for school and when I need to leave for work. I could just sit down and do it as soon as the kids leave.

T: Let's try it. Can you put the times down in your appointment book?

C: Sure.

T: Why don't you try this out for homework? It might seem very difficult at first because you aren't used to doing things in this way. Try to stick with it, though. If you run into difficulties, try writing them down and bring them to next week's session. Does that sound good?

C: Sure. I'll give it a try.

Module 2
Reducing Distractibility

Session 6 | *Gauging Attention Span and Distractibility Delay*

(Corresponds to Chapter 8 of the Client Workbook)

Materials Needed

- Symptom Severity Scale
- Clock or stopwatch

Session Outline

- Set agenda
- Review symptom severity scale
- Review medication adherence
- Review progress
- Review use of calendar, task list, and work from previous module
- Teach client to gauge his attention span, and develop a plan for breaking tasks down into steps that take a corresponding length of time
- Teach client to implement the distractibility delay
- Assign homework

Set Agenda

It is important to begin each session by setting an agenda. Review the session outline with the client.

Review of Symptom Severity Scale

Per usual, the client completes the ADHD self-report symptom checklist at the beginning of the session. Briefly review the score and take note of symptoms that have improved and those that are still problematic.

Score: _____

Date: _____

Review of Medication Adherence

Each week the client records his prescribed dosage of medication and indicates the number of doses that were missed during the week. Assist the client in identifying triggers for missed doses, such as distractibility, running out of medication, or thoughts about not wanting/needing to take medication. Problem-solve as necessary to increase adherence.

Prescribed doses per week: _____

Doses missed this week: _____

Triggers for missed doses: _____

_____   _____

Review of Previous Modules

Using the tools below, review the client's progress practicing and implementing skills from each of the previous modules. It is important to acknowledge the successes the client has achieved and to problem-solve around any difficulties.

■ **Calendar for managing appointments:** Assess whether the client has begun to use a calendar book. Some clients want to get started using a new, electronic system, such as a Palm Pilot. *If they have not been able to figure out how to use it, it is important to have a discussion about how realistic using an electronic calendar system will be.* Discuss how frequently the client uses the book, making sure that she looks at the calendar daily. Finally, discuss any problems that the client is having with using the calendar system.

■ **Notebook for recording a to-do list:** Review any difficulties that the client is having writing down and using the to-do list on a daily basis. Emphasize the importance of looking at and using the to-do list each and every day.

■ **Use of the "A," "B," and "C" priority ratings:** If the client is having any trouble with prioritizing tasks, discuss at this point.

■ **Use of problem-solving (selecting an action plan and breaking down large tasks into small steps):** Consider the client's use of these strategies, and practice one or both skills using examples from her current task list.

Introduction

Clients with ADHD commonly report that they are unable to complete tasks because other, less important tasks or distractions get in the way. Having a short attention span is part of ADHD. We do not view having a short attention span as being associated with a lack of intelligence or ability. Rather, it suggests that people with ADHD need to use extra skills in order to cope.

Gauging the Client's Attention Span

The purpose of this exercise is to help clients estimate the length of time that they can work on a boring or unattractive task without stopping.

Either give the client a clock or stopwatch or instruct the client to buy one. In session, instruct the client to choose a boring or unattractive task to work on for homework. After starting the task, the client should keep track of how long she can work before taking a break or becoming distracted. The client should note this length of time and repeat this exercise several times to see if a consistent "attention span" emerges.

The next strategy is to help the client use problem-solving skills to break important tasks down into small steps that they can do within their attention span. You can discuss the fact that the client will be learning additional skills to help gradually increase the length of his attention span.

Implementing the Distractibility Delay

The distractibility delay is an exercise that can be done in addition to the strategies described earlier. It is similar to an exercise used in anxiety-disorder treatments (e.g., Craske, Barlow, & Meadows, 2000) and can be used as a strategy for delaying attending to distractions while working on boring or unattractive tasks.

Instruct the client to have the notebook on hand when starting work on a boring or unattractive task. Then, set a timer for the length of his attention span (or possibly slightly longer). When a distraction pops into his head, the client should write the distracting thought down in the notebook but not take action at that time. Instead, the client should return to the task at hand. When the timer goes off, the client can look at the list and decide if any of the distracting tasks need to be completed at that time.

Instruct the client to repeat this process until the task (or the portion of the task that the client has set out to do for the day) is completed. The client can then review the list of distractions and decide if they need to be completed at that time, if they should be added to the client's to-do list, or if they are unimportant tasks that do not need to be completed.

Also, explain to the client that she can use coping statements to help her return to the task at hand. These can include "I will worry about this later," "This is not an A-priority task," or "I will come back to this."

Potential Pitfalls

Clients may become frustrated if they aren't able to immediately implement the distractibility delay and/or increase the length of their attention span. Clients should be encouraged to look at this as a process that may take a while to perfect. They should be reminded that it took them many years to develop their old habits, and it is not realistic to expect that they can change overnight.

Homework

- Start using problem-solving to break down boring tasks into "chunks" that fit the length of the client's attention span.
- Use the distractibility delay technique when working on aversive or boring tasks.
- Use the notebook every day to review active to-do list.
- Rate each task as an "A," "B," or "C" task.
- Practice doing all of the "A" tasks before the "B" tasks and all of the "B" tasks before the "C" tasks.
- Use problem-solving skills (selection of action plan, breaking down tasks into steps as needed).
- Keep up with using triage center to sort bills, papers, and mail.
- Keep up with filing important papers in filing system.

Case Vignette

C: I'm not sure if I will be able to do the distractibility delay. I'm so used to doing things as soon as the idea strikes me.

T: Well, does that usually work for you?

C: No, not really. I usually start things and then I go off and start doing other things and I forget what I was even working on in the first place.

T: So, do you think it makes sense to try a different strategy?

C: I guess so.

T: Well, what's the worst thing that could happen if you try the distractibility delay technique?

C: I could feel really uncomfortable when I just write down the distraction but don't do it right away.

T: Do you think you could tolerate this?

C: I guess so.

T: Do you want to give it a try.

C: Okay. It's worth a shot.

Session 7 | *Modifying the Environment*

(Corresponds to Chapter 9 of the Client Workbook)

Materials Needed

- Symptoms Severity Scale
- Form: Strategies for Reducing Distractions
- Colored dot stickers
- Alarm device

Session Outline

- Set agenda
- Review symptom severity scale
- Review medication adherence
- Review progress
- Review use of calendar, task list, problem-solving strategies, and work from previous module
- Teach client strategies for controlling her work environment
- Teach client skills for keeping track of important objects
- Teach client to use reminders to help with skill consolidation
- Instruct client in use of alarm device to help with staying on task
- Assign homework

Set Agenda

It is important to begin each session by setting an agenda. Review the session outline with the client.

Review of Symptom Severity Scale

Per usual, the client completes the ADHD self-report symptom checklist at the beginning of the session. Briefly review the score and take note of symptoms that have improved and those that are still problematic.

Score: _____

Date: _____

Review of Medication Adherence

Each week the client records her prescribed dosage of medication and indicates the number of doses that were missed during the week. Assist the client in identifying triggers for missed doses, such as distractibility, running out of medication, or thoughts about not wanting/needing to take medication. Problem-solve as necessary to increase adherence.

Prescribed doses per week: _____

Doses missed this week: _____

Triggers for missed doses: _____

_____

_____

Review of Previous Modules

Review the client's progress implementing skills from each of the previous modules. It is important to acknowledge the successes the client has achieved and to problem-solve around any difficulties.

Review: Tools for Organization and Planning

- **Calendar for managing appointments:** At this point, you should discuss any problems that the client is having using the calendar system.

- **Notebook for recording a to-do list:** Review any difficulties that the client is having with writing down and using the to-do list on a daily basis.

- **Use of the "A," "B," and "C" priority ratings:** If the client is having any trouble with prioritizing tasks, they should be discussed at this point.

- **Use of problem-solving (selecting an action plan and breaking down large tasks into small steps):** Consider the client's use of these strategies, and practice one or both skills using examples from his current task list.

Review: Tools for Reducing Distractibility

- **Breaking boring tasks down into manageable chunks:** At this point, you should discuss any problems that the client is having breaking down boring tasks into manageable chunks.

- **Use of the distractibility delay:** Review any difficulties that the client is having with the distractibility delay technique.

Controlling the Work Environment

It is important for individuals with ADHD to work in an environment that has few distractions. Even with the coping with distractibility skills discussed earlier, most people are somewhat distractible when they are trying to concentrate. Sometimes, distractions interfere to the point that it is too difficult to get things done.

Instruct the client to think about the things that typically are distracting while working. These may include the ringing of the telephone, surfing the Internet, replying to e-mails or instant messages, listening to the radio, watching television, noticing other things on the desk that require attention, speaking with other people in the room, or looking at something going on outside the window.

Using the Strategies for Reducing Distractions form, help the client develop a plan for reducing the distractions that are problematic. Strategies can include turning off the phone, closing the web browser and/or e-mail, shutting off the noise that beeps when a new e-mail arrives, clearing off the desk or workspace, turning off the radio and television, asking others not to come in while the client is working, and turning the client's desk away from the window.

Instruct the client to find one place in his home where he can do important tasks without distraction. It could be a desk or a table or any other work space.

Keeping Track of Important Objects

One hallmark symptom of ADHD is frequently losing important items. This is problematic because it can cause clients to be late and increase feelings of frustration. Ask the client to think of any difficulties that she has keeping track of important objects such as keys, wallet, notebook, appointment book, or Palm Pilot. The client should pay special attention to those items that are needed each time that she leaves the house.

Next, instruct the client to think of a specific place in the house where these objects will be kept. This can include such strategies as leaving a basket near the door and placing the important objects in the basket each time that the client comes in the door or installing a hanging rack next to the door for keys. The client should be encouraged to think of one or more solutions that are likely to be effective.

Instruct the client to involve other family members in the process. If everyone in the household is aware of where things belong, family members can be helpful in reminding the client to put things away if they notice that something is out of place. Also, emphasize the importance of placing the item in the appropriate place immediately, as soon as the client notices something out of place.

Form: Strategies for Reducing Distractions

Distraction	Environmental Reduction Strategy

Using Reminders

Another strategy for managing distractibility is to use reminders to cue clients to use their skills. We recommend using colored adhesive dots. These dots can be placed on items that are often distracting, such as the telephone, the computer, the radio, the window, and the refrigerator. The dots should be placed in such a way that they are visible to the client.

Each time that the client sees an adhesive dot, he should ask himself the following questions: "Am I doing what I am supposed to be doing or did I get distracted?" and "Am I using my skills for ADHD right now?" Clients should be instructed that if they discover that they have become distracted or are off-task, they should return to the task at hand immediately.

Using an Alarm Device

An alarm device can be helpful to prompt the client to check in with herself on a regular basis about whether or not she is on-task. An alarm clock or an alarm on the client's watch, Palm Pilot, computer, or cell phone can be used for this purpose.

In our research into this program, we provided individuals with watches with alarms. However, you can instruct the client to purchase one and set the alarm to go off at regularly scheduled intervals. Many watches have a feature that allow them to go off each hour. We, however, recommend trying to have the alarm sound each half-hour, especially during times when the client is trying to be productive.

When the alarm sounds, the client should to ask herself, "Am I doing what I am supposed to be doing, or did I get distracted?" If the client notices that she has become distracted, she should be instructed to immediately return to the task at hand.

Potential Pitfalls

It is easy to get frustrated with these strategies if they don't work right away. Remind clients that they are trying to develop new work habits and that this takes time. Encourage them to think about the long-term benefits of learning new work habits.

Homework

- Start using problem-solving to break down boring tasks into "chunks" that fit the length of the client's attention span.

- Use the distractibility delay technique when working on aversive or boring tasks.

- Use notebook every day to review active to-do list.

- Rate each task as an "A," "B," or "C" task.

- Practice doing all of the "A" tasks before the "B" tasks and all of the "B" tasks before the "C" tasks.

- Use problem-solving skills (selection of action plan, breaking down tasks into steps as needed).

- Keep up with using triage center to sort bills, papers, and mail.

- Keep up with filing important papers in filing system.

- Use the distractibility delay technique when working on aversive or boring tasks.

- Use skills to reduce distractions in work environment.

- Start putting important objects in specific places.

- Use the colored dots as reminders for client to check in with herself to see if she has become distracted.

- Use alarm to remind client to check in with herself to see if she has become distracted.

T: I want you to take these colored dots and place them in several places where you typically get distracted during the day.

C: Where should I put them?

T: Well, that depends. Where do you think you experience the most difficulty with distractibility?

C: I have a lot of trouble when I am sitting at my computer at work. I get very easily distracted by e-mail, and sometimes when I really don't want to do work, I start playing solitaire or other computer games.

T: Okay, then I would suggest that you place one on your computer where it will catch your eye. Every time that you see the colored dot, you should ask yourself, "Am I on-task right now, or did I get distracted?" What other situations are difficult for you?

C: If something is going on outside my window, I have a hard time ignoring it. Sometimes I will just stare out the window for 15 or 20 minutes before I catch myself.

T: Then I would suggest that you put another dot on your window. When you notice the dot, you can quickly remind yourself to get back to work on the task at hand.

Module 3
Adaptive Thinking

Session 8 — *Introduction to a Cognitive Model of ADHD*

(Corresponds to Chapter 10 of the Client Workbook)

Materials Needed

- Symptom Severity Scale
- Three copies of blank three-column Thought Records
- Seven copies of blank four-column Thought Records
- Form: List of Thinking Errors
- Form: Preliminary Instructions for Adaptive Thinking

Session Outline

- Set agenda
- Review Symptom Severity Scale
- Review medication adherence
- Review homework from previous modules
- Introduce the cognitive component of the cognitive-behavioral model of ADHD
- Discuss automatic thinking and the relationship of thoughts to behaviors and feelings
- Explain how to identify negative thoughts
- Introduce the three-column Thought Record
- Introduce the list of thinking errors

- Discuss labeling thinking errors (four-column Thought Record)
- Assign homework

Set Agenda

It is important to begin each session by setting an agenda. Review the session outline with the client.

Review Symptom Severity Scale

Each week the client completes the ADHD self-report symptom checklist at the beginning of the session. Review the total score, and engage the client in a discussion about symptoms that have improved and those that are still problematic. It is helpful to keep all checklists organized in the client's file so that you may review previous scores as needed.

Score: _____

Date: _____

Review of Medication Adherence

Each week the client records his prescribed dosage of medication and indicates the number of doses that were missed during the week. Assist the client in identifying triggers for missed doses, such as distractibility, running out of medication, or thoughts about not wanting/needing to take medication. Problem-solve as necessary to increase adherence.

Prescribed doses per week: _____

Doses missed this week: _____

Triggers for missed doses: _____

_____

_____

Each session will also begin with a review of clients' progress implementing skills from each of the previous modules. It is important to acknowledge successes and to problem-solve any difficulties they may be having. It is okay to spend a large portion of the session reviewing homework, as long as you allow enough time to introduce new materials. Repetition of new skills is critical for individuals with ADHD and will maximize gains made in treatment and increase the likelihood of sustaining improvement.

Review: Tools for Organization and Planning

- Calendar for managing appointments
- Notebook for recording a to-do list
- Notebook for breaking tasks down into subtasks
- Notebook for managing and prioritizing multiple tasks
- Strategies for problem-solving and developing an action plan
- Triage and filing systems

Review: Strategies for Reducing Distractibility

- Breaking tasks down to match duration of attention span and taking breaks between tasks
- Utilizing distractibility delay
- Removing distractions from the environment
- Identifying a specific place for each important object
- Distractibility reminders (dots and alarm): "Am I doing what I am supposed to be doing?"

By now, you have worked with your client to develop systems for organizing, planning, and problem-solving and to practice skills for managing distractibility. The next section, adaptive thinking, teaches clients to increase their awareness of negative thoughts that can cause stress and mood problems and can interfere with the successful completion of tasks.

This method of learning to think adaptively has been used in similar cognitive-behavioral treatments and has been effective in treating many other psychological disorders such as depression and anxiety disorders.[1] The major goal of learning to think about tasks and situations adaptively is to reduce the number of times that negative thoughts or moods interfere with tasks or follow-through, cause distress, or add to distractibility. Your aim is to communicate the message that the previously learned strategies can be impeded by negative thoughts. However, your client can learn strategies for removing these barriers and thereby more effectively manage symptoms of ADHD.

Adaptive thinking will enable clients to:

- Increase their awareness of negative, interfering thoughts

- Develop strategies for keeping thoughts in check

- Minimize symptoms

Adaptive thinking is important because of the interrelationship among thoughts, feelings, and behaviors. This model emphasizes the important connection between thoughts, feelings, and behaviors in a given situation. The cognitive part of cognitive-behavioral therapy refers to the fact that thoughts contribute to how people act and feel.

---

[1] This method of implementing and teaching cognitive-restructuring skills is based on McDermott (2000), as well as other CBT therapy manuals, including Hope et al.'s (2000) manual for the treatment of social phobia and the Otto et al. (1996) manual for treatment of panic disorder in the context of medication discontinuation.

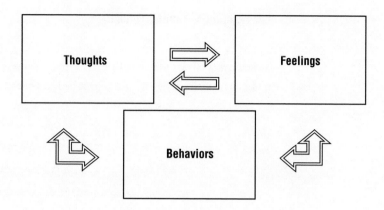

The Cognitive Component of Treatment: Automatic Thinking

The goal of this section is to highlight the role of negative thoughts in ADHD symptoms. First discuss the automatic nature of thoughts. Some thoughts happen so quickly that they are not in one's present awareness. Furthermore, automatic thoughts can be detrimental when they are characterized by negative content. What follows is a suggested dialogue:

In the course of a given day, numerous thoughts go through your mind. What is surprising is that often you are not aware of these thoughts. However, they play an important role in determining how you are feeling in a situation and how you may respond. When you are feeling overwhelmed or stressed or are anticipating completing a task, the thoughts that go through your mind play a critical role in determining the outcome of your situation.

These thoughts are "automatic"—they happen on their own. For example, think about when you first learned to drive a car. In order to coordinate many tasks at once, you had to be conscious of handling the steering wheel, remembering to signal for turns, staying exactly in your lane, averting other traffic, and trying to park. You were doing many tasks at the same time that required your total attention.

Now, think about driving today. You probably know how to drive without actively thinking about what you are doing. You likely don't even remember thinking about all of these steps because they have become automatic.

Less Helpful Automatic Thinking

Sometimes, clients don't realize that their negative thoughts actually make their task harder. To make this point, consider the following dialogue:

In many situations, automatic thoughts enable us to complete a task more easily. Unfortunately, in other situations, automatic thoughts interfere with achieving goals. For example, imagine you have to do task you will probably not enjoy, such as preparing your tax return. Imagine the following types of thoughts going through your mind:

> *"I am careless and am going to do this wrong."*
>
> *"This is going to take forever."*
>
> *"If I complete my return, I will realize I owe money."*
>
> *"If I owe money, I am going to not have enough for rent."*

If these thoughts are going through your head, then you can easily see that this task will feel overwhelming and stressful. This will increase the chance that you will procrastinate by doing any other possible task.

Relationship of Thoughts to Feelings and Behaviors

To help your client understand why it is important to identify and change maladaptive thinking, discuss the relationship between automatic thinking and behavioral outcome, usually some form of avoidance. Negative automatic thoughts about a situation can cause a person avoid the situation because he (1) feels worse and (2) expects the outcome of the situation to be negative. Avoidance can lead to more anxiety, restlessness, and perhaps irritability or depression, because the task doesn't get done, and then the person feels even worse about it.

Anxiety and depression may lead to more negative thinking, and around and around the cycle goes, making the problem worse and worse. For people with ADHD, this cycle exacerbates other symptoms, such as inattention, procrastination, frustration, and depression.

The first step in breaking this cycle is to identify and slow down negative, automatic thinking. Becoming more aware of situations when this occurs is the first step in learning to think in more adaptive ways.

Skill: Identifying Negative Automatic Thoughts

The Thought Record is a tool that was developed to help clients learn how to identify, slow down, and restructure negative automatic thoughts. Clients may use the forms provided or their notebook by drawing in the columns and respective headings. Complete one Thought Record in session with clients to make sure they understand how it is done. Ask clients to identify one distressing situation they experienced in the past week or a time when they felt overwhelmed, stressed, sad, or upset.

It is important to have the client write out the Thought Record (not the therapist) so that she becomes more familiar with the format of the worksheet. The Thought Record should be completed by the client as follows:

Ask the client to write a brief description of the **situation** in **Column 1**. When did it take place? Where was he? With whom? What was going on? Ideally, the description of the situation should be a sentence or two at most.

Then, instruct the client to write down all of her **automatic thoughts** in **Column 2**. What was going through her mind at the time? What was she saying to herself about the situation? Other people? Her role in the situation? What was she afraid might happen? What is the worst thing that could happen if this is true? What does this mean about how the other person feels/thinks about her?

(Note: When coming up with automatic thoughts, it is important to help clients separate thoughts from feelings. Gently instruct clients that thoughts are ideas going through their mind during the situation; feelings go in the next column.)

Next, ask the client to list all of the **feelings** she experienced in **Column 3** (there may be several different feelings) and then to rate the **intensity** of each feeling on a scale of 0–100 (0 = the least intense, 100 = the most intense). Examples of feelings include angry, upset, happy, sad, depressed, anxious, surprised. You can show the client the following sample if necessary. Provide a blank three-column Thought Record for in-session practice.

Example: Three-Column Thought Record

Time and Situation	Automatic Thoughts	Mood and Intensity
At home, thinking about doing my taxes	This is going to be so much work. I am never going to finish them. I am never going to find everything I need to. I am going to get audited. I am going to end up having to pay so much money.	Overwhelmed (80) Anxious (75) Frustrated (80)

Introduce Thinking Errors

Now that clients see how certain situations can trigger negative automatic thoughts and subsequent negative feelings, our goal is to help them understand why their thoughts are unhelpful and to recognize errors in thinking. In our experience, and in the work of other cognitive-behavioral therapists, common types of negative automatic thoughts often emerge. These types of thoughts may interfere with clients' ability to complete tasks and also contribute to feelings of depression, anxiety, or frustration.

What follows is a list of common thinking errors, taken from Heimberg (1991), with some modifications. (Heimberg [1991] was in turn based on Persons [1989].) Review each error with clients to make sure they understand them all. Help them look for patterns and determine which types of errors may be especially problematic for them.

All-or-nothing thinking: You see things in black-and-white categories—for example, ALL aspects of a project need to be completed immediately, or, if your performance falls short of perfect, you see it as a total failure.

Overgeneralization: You see a single negative event as part of a never-ending pattern.

Mental filter: You pick out a single negative detail and dwell on it exclusively, overlooking other, positive aspects of the situation.

Disqualifying the positive: You reject positive experiences by insisting they "don't count" for some reason or other. In this way, you can maintain a negative belief that is contradicted by your everyday experiences.

Jumping to conclusions: You make a negative interpretation even though there are no facts that convincingly support your conclusion.

> *Mind reading:* You arbitrarily conclude that someone is reacting negatively to you, and you don't bother to check this out.

> *Fortune telling:* You anticipate that things will turn out badly, and you feel that your prediction is a predetermined fact.

Magnification/minimization: You exaggerate the importance of things (such as your mistake or someone else's achievement), or you inappropriately shrink things until they appear tiny (your own desirable qualities or the other's imperfections).

Catastrophizing: You attribute extreme and horrible consequences to the outcomes of events. One mistake at work is the same as being fired from your job.

Emotional reasoning: You assume that your negative emotions necessarily reflect the way things really are: "I feel it, so it must be true."

"Should" statements: You try to motivate yourself with "shoulds" and "shouldn'ts," as if you need to be punished before you can be expected to do anything. With regard to others, you feel anger, frustration, and resentment.

Labeling and mislabeling: This is an extreme form of overgeneralization. Instead of describing an error, you attach a broad negative label to yourself or others.

Personalization: You see negative events as indicative of some negative characteristic of yourself or others, or you take responsibility for events that were not your doing.

Maladaptive thinking: You focus on a thought that may be true but over which you have no control. Excessively focusing on one thought can be a form of self-criticism and can distract you from an important task or from attempting new behaviors.

After clients have learned about common types of thinking errors, go back to the Thought Record they filled out with you earlier. For each of the automatic thoughts they listed, review the list of thinking errors and help them identify the common patterns in their thinking. Then, list the appropriate thinking error in **Column 4** in the four-column Thought Record. Sometimes more than one thinking error is made, and there may be some overlap among different types of errors.

 It is important to remind clients that not all negative thoughts represent thinking errors. Sometimes it is realistic for a situation to produce a negative thought, which in turn contributes to a negative feeling. We offer the following example to illustrate this:

Imagine you had studied for an exam for many days, and you were driving to school to take the exam. Then, suddenly you encountered a traffic jam caused by a car accident that had occurred earlier. Now, if your thought was "Oh no, I hope I won't be late. I studied so hard for this exam," and you were feeling anxious and perhaps frustrated, that would make sense! The challenge for you would be to problem-solve—try to stay calm, perhaps call the instructor to let her know that you were going to be late, and focus on driving safely.

However, if in addition to those thoughts you also said to yourself, "Bad things always happen to me, I can never do anything right, I am going to miss the exam and fail the class," we can imagine that your anxiety and despair would intensify, and you might be more likely to drive dangerously, get in an accident, and not be able to take the exam. Furthermore, if you did get to the exam in time, you most likely would be distracted by these intense emotions and would be less able to concentrate compared to when you were studying. Looking closely, you can see that these thoughts, respectively, could be classified as overgeneralization, personalization, and jumping to conclusions.

Refer to the following example and then provide clients with copies of the four-column Thought Record to complete on their own.

Example: Four-Column Thought Record

Time and Situation	Automatic Thoughts	Mood and Intensity	Thinking Error
Preparing a report for work	I have to do all of this today.	Overwhelmed (80)	All-or-nothing thinking
	I must do this perfectly.	Anxious (75)	All-or-nothing thinking
	If I do not finish my boss will be upset.	Depressed (60)	Jumping to conclusions (mind reading)
	If the project is not perfect and my boss is upset, I will lose my job.		Jumping to conclusions (fortune telling), catastrophizing

Potential Pitfalls

Often, clients feel that it is impossible to change how they think. It is important to acknowledge that change does not occur overnight, but clinical experience and research suggest that it is possible! Sometimes monitoring thoughts alone can begin the process of change. For especially skeptical clients, it can be helpful to suggest they do an experiment: For the next month, they will commit to using Thought Records to monitor their thoughts, label unhelpful thoughts, and attempt to identify more rational responses. If at the end of this one-month experiment they detect absolutely no change, they may consider returning to their dialogue of negative thoughts. However, chances are that with consistent monitoring and practice, they will begin to see improvement.

For some people, writing out negative thoughts makes the thoughts "seem more real" or more difficult to cope with. Because of this, they are reluctant to utilize Thought Records. However, the thought is in their mind, interfering, regardless of whether or not they write it down. Completing the Thought Record will actually help them feel better about the situation, despite the initial difficulty of seeing their thought on paper.

Clients may also find that it is hard to label their feeling(s) and may think that they have to come up with the perfect words to describe their feelings. Ask them to use the first word that comes to mind, even if it is not perfect. Over time, it will become easier to label their feelings.

- Continue utilizing and reviewing skills from previous modules.

- Read the forms on Preliminary Instructions for Adaptive Thinking and identifying thinking errors.

- Complete Thought Records for at least two situations during the week.

As was emphasized in previous modules, instructing clients to practice new skills is vital so that they become familiar with them, are able to easily use the tools, and begin to see the positive results that can emerge when they *consistently* use these CBT strategies. Remind clients that, at first, when they are learning a new skill, it may feel awkward, may be confusing, and may require effort to implement. That's okay! The more they practice, the easier it will become.

In this session, try to anticipate which situations they may want to work on in the upcoming week. In addition, be sure to anticipate any problems that may get in the way of completing the homework. For example, having a busy schedule, going out of town, or being uncertain about how to complete an assignment may make it more difficult for clients to practice skills. We have found that if clients can work with their therapist to anticipate and problem-solve in advance, these obstacles can become manageable, and clients will be more likely to achieve success with the new skills.

Also, remind clients that they do not have to complete these home assignments perfectly. The idea is for them to begin monitoring the thoughts that arise in difficult situations and to begin practicing identifying the common types of thinking errors.

Case Vignette

T: Let's practice completing a Thought Record together, and then you will be able to work on them at home this week

C: To be honest, I really don't see how writing down my thoughts is going to change anything. I'm not always going to have a Thought Record with me that I can complete when I run into problems.

(an example of resistance to completing assignments)

T: Those are really good points. Many people actually aren't sure how Thought Records can be helpful until they start practicing. What we find is that seeing your thoughts on paper helps you identify when they are unrealistic and highlights the connection between unhelpful, negative thoughts and feelings like anxiety, which can lead to procrastination. Also, I don't expect that you will always need to complete Thought Records. Over time, with lots of practice, you will start to catch yourself having negative thoughts and will restructure them in your mind. The whole process will become automatic. But for now, while you are learning, it is helpful to slow down the process and write out a Thought Record.

(acknowledges client's concerns but gently encourages the client to practice for a while and then determine if the feared outcome actually occurs)

C: I guess that makes sense. Let's just see what happens.

T: Good. Can you think of a situation in which you were experiencing negative feelings from this past week?

C: Yes. I got a notice in the mail from my bank requesting copies of my last six pay stubs because there was an error with my direct deposit. I have been really anxious and worried about it and haven't been able to respond to them all week.

T: Okay. So let's write down the situation in the first column. Next, can you identify some of the thoughts that were going through your mind when you got the notice?

(the therapist takes a matter-of-fact approach and begins to break down the situation into the appropriate columns)

C: I really freaked out. I don't want them to take back any money.

T: Then let's write down your thought "I don't want them to take back any money" in the next column. Were there any other thoughts running through your mind?

C: Yes. I don't even know where my pay stubs are. This is such a pain in the neck. I shouldn't have to spend time doing this stuff.

T: Okay. Let's write all these thoughts down. You said you freaked out. What were feeling at the time?

(the therapist assists the client in distinguishing between thoughts and feelings)

C: I was anxious, overwhelmed, annoyed, worried. . . .

T: Good. You're doing a great job breaking down this difficult situation. Can you rate those feelings on a scale of 0–100?

C: Um, anxious 85, overwhelmed 100, annoyed 70, worried 90.

T: Okay, now let's take a look at the list of thinking errors. Do you think it makes sense to have these thoughts you described, or do any of them fall under the categories listed here?

C: Well, I really don't know where the pay stubs are, this really is a pain in the neck, and if it's their error, I shouldn't have to waste my time fixing it. And if they take back my money I won't be able to pay my rent, and my landlord will evict me if I'm late one more time.

(here the intensity of emotion increases and the client begins to feel worried again)

T: Now wait a minute. Do you think there is any "Jumping to Conclusions" going on? You have no way of knowing for sure that they are going to take your money back, and chances are that if there is an error, it will not affect the entire amount you were paid. And maybe there is some "Magnification/Minimization"—focusing on the fact that you don't know where the pay stubs are but minimizing the fact that it is usually possible to get duplicate copies when you get to work. I agree, it is a pain in the neck, and it makes sense you would be frustrated.

(the therapist validates the client's concerns and calmly suggest thinking errors that may be contributing to the client's anxiety and worry)

C: I guess that makes sense. When you break it down like that, it doesn't seem so overwhelming, and I know it would just take a phone call to get new copies sent right to the bank.

T: Exactly. You've done a terrific job. This is a great example of how using the Thought Record can help you see a situation from a new perspective, which can really have an impact on how you're feeling about it. Otherwise, your intense feelings may get in the way of taking necessary action.

(the therapist provides praise and reinforcement for the client's efforts)

C: That was a lot of work, but I guess it will be worth practicing.

T: You will also find that it gets much easier the more you practice.

Form: Three-Column Thought Record

Time and Situation	Automatic Thoughts	Mood and Intensity

Form: Four-Column Thought Record

Time and Situation	Automatic Thoughts	Mood and Intensity	Thinking Error

The purpose of using Thought Records is to identify and modify negative automatic thoughts in situations that lead to feeling overwhelmed.

The first step in learning to think in more useful ways is to become more aware of these thoughts and their relationship to your feelings. If you are anticipating a stressful situation or a task that is making you feel overwhelmed, write out your thoughts regarding this situation.

If a situation has already passed and you find that you are thinking about it negatively, list your thoughts for this situation.

The **first column** is a description of the situation.

The **second column** is for you to list your thoughts during a stressful, overwhelming, or uncontrollable situation.

The **third column** is for you to write down what emotions or feelings you are having when thinking these thoughts (e.g., depressed, sad, angry).

The **fourth column** is for you to see if your thoughts match the list of "thinking errors." These may include:

- All-or-nothing thinking

- Overgeneralizations

- Jumping to conclusions: fortune telling/mind reading

- Magnification/minimization

- Emotional reasoning

- "Should" statements

- Labeling and mislabeling

- Personalization

- Maladaptive thinking

Session 9   *Adaptive Thinking*

(Corresponds to Chapter 11 of the Client Workbook)

Materials Needed

- Symptom Severity Scale
- Seven copies of blank Thought Records
- Coaching Story
- Form: Adaptive Thinking

Session Outline

- Set agenda
- Review Symptom Severity Scale
- Review medication adherence
- Review homework from previous modules
- Review Thought Records completed at home
- Discuss coaching styles and coaching story
- Discuss formulation of a rational response
- Assign homework

Set Agenda

It is important to begin each session by setting an agenda to maintain a structured focus on treatment for ADHD and prepare the client for what lies ahead in the upcoming session. Use the session outline to set the agenda.

Review of Symptom Severity Scale

As always, the client completes the ADHD self-report symptom checklist at the beginning of the session. Review the total score and engage the client in a discussion about symptoms that have improved and those that are still problematic. It is helpful to keep all checklists organized in the client's file so that you may review previous scores as needed.

Score: _____

Date: _____

Review of Medication Adherence

Each week the client records her prescribed dosage of medication and indicates the number of doses that were missed during the week. Assist the client in identifying triggers for missed doses, such as distractibility, running out of medication, or thoughts about not wanting/needing to take medication. Problem-solve as necessary to increase adherence.

Prescribed doses per week: _____

Doses missed this week: _____

Triggers for missed doses: _____

_____

_____

Review the client's progress implementing skills from each of the previous modules. It is important to acknowledge the successes he has achieved and to problem-solve around any difficulties he may be having. Remember, repetition of new skills is critical for individuals with ADHD and will maximize gains made in treatment.

Review: Tools for Organization and Planning

■ Calendar for managing appointments

■ Notebook for recording a to-do list

■ Notebook for breaking tasks down into subtasks

■ Notebook for managing and prioritizing multiple tasks

■ Strategies for problem-solving and developing an action plan

■ Triage and filing systems

Review: Strategies for Reducing Distractibility

■ Breaking tasks down to match duration of attention span and taking breaks between tasks

■ Utilizing distractibility delay

■ Removing distractions from the environment

■ Utilizing stimulus control—identifying a specific place for each important object

■ Distractibility reminders (dots and alarm): "Am I doing what I am supposed to be doing?"

Review: Adaptive Thinking

■ Using the Thought Record to identify and label automatic thoughts

Review the Thought Records the client completed at home. If she was not able to complete any Thought Records, try to identify the obstacles that may have interfered, and utilize the problem-solving skills to determine the best way for her to work on automatic thinking. Did she have difficulty making time for home practice? Were the directions confusing? Was it difficult to see her thoughts in writing? It is possible to try to work with the client on "rethinking" the situation in her head versus on paper. We have found that writing out the automatic thoughts helps people "step back" from their thought and better identify the difference between thoughts and emotions; however, in reality, it can sometimes be difficult to get patients with ADHD to write these out on paper.

If the client didn't do any home practice, work on a Thought Record together before moving on.

If the client did complete Thought Records, review each one. Provide feedback on successful completion, and assist the client in identifying any patterns to negative thoughts. Often, clients have a tendency toward a particular thinking error. Once it is recognized, the client can begin to modify his thoughts.

Skill: Formulating a Rational Response

In this session, the client will learn strategies for correcting thinking errors and developing more helpful thoughts. Our goal is to help transform the unhelpful interfering thoughts into more supportive coaching thoughts. In order to understand how powerful thoughts can be, we tell the following coaching story (taken from Otto, 2000).

This is a story about Little League baseball. I talk about Little League baseball because of the amazing parents and coaches involved. And by "amazing" I don't mean good. I mean extreme.

But this story doesn't start with the coaches or the parents; it starts with Johnny, who is a Little League player in the outfield. His job is to catch "fly balls" and return them to the infield players. On this particular day of our story, Johnny is in the outfield. And "crack!"—one of the players on the other team hits a fly ball. The ball is coming to Johnny. Johnny raises his glove. The ball is coming to him, it is coming to him . . . and it goes over his head. Johnny misses the ball, and the other team scores a run.

Now there are a number of ways a coach can respond to this situation. Let's take Coach A first. Coach A is the type of coach who will come out on the field and shout: "I can't believe you missed that ball! Anyone could have caught it! My dog could have caught it! You screw up like that again and you'll be sitting on the bench! That was lousy!"

Coach A then storms off the field. At this point, if Johnny is anything like I am, he is standing there, tense, tight, trying not to cry, and praying that another ball is not hit to him. If a ball does come to him, Johnny will probably miss it. After all, he is tense, tight, and he may see four balls coming to him because of the tears in his eyes. Also, if we are Johnny's parents, we may see more profound changes after the game: Johnny, who typically places his baseball glove on the mantle, now throws it under his bed. And before the next game, he may complain that his stomach hurts, that perhaps he should not go to the game. This is the scenario with Coach A.

Now let's go back to the original event and play it differently. Johnny has just missed the fly ball, and now Coach B comes out on the field. Coach B says: "Well, you missed that one. Here is what I want you to remember: fly balls always look like they are farther away than they really are. Also, it is much easier to run forward than to back up. Because of this, I want you to prepare for the ball by taking a few extra steps backwards. Run forward if you need to, but try to catch it at chest level, so you can adjust your hand if you misjudge the ball. Let's see how you do next time."

Coach B leaves the field. How does Johnny feel? Well, he is not happy. After all, he missed the ball—but there are a number of important differences from the way he felt with Coach A. He is not as tense or tight, and if a fly ball does come to him, he knows what to do differently to catch it. And because he does not have tears in his eyes, he may actually see the ball accurately. He may catch the next one.

So, if we were the type of parent that eventually wants Johnny to make the major leagues, we would pick Coach B, because he teaches Johnny how to be a more effective player. Johnny knows what to do differently, may catch more balls, and may excel at the game. But if we don't care whether Johnny makes the major leagues—because baseball is a game, and one is supposed to be able to enjoy a game—then we would still pick Coach B. We pick Coach B because we care whether Johnny enjoys the game. With Coach B, Johnny knows what to do differently; he is not tight, tense, and ready to cry; he may catch a few balls; and he may enjoy the game. And he may continue to place his glove on the mantel.

Now, while we may all select Coach B for Johnny, we rarely choose the view of Coach B for the way we talk to ourselves. Think about your last mistake. Did you say, "I can't believe I did that! I am so stupid! What a jerk!" These are "Coach A" thoughts, and they have approximately the same effect on us as they do on Johnny. They make us feel tense and tight and sometimes make us feel like crying. And this style of coaching rarely makes us do better in the future. Even if you are concerned only about productivity (making the major leagues), you would still pick Coach B. And if you were concerned with enjoying life, while guiding yourself effectively for both joy and productivity, you would still pick Coach B.

Keep in mind that we are not talking about how we coach ourselves in a baseball game. We are talking about how we coach ourselves in life, and our enjoyment of life.

During the next week, I would like you to listen to see how you are coaching yourself. And if you hear Coach A, remember this story and see if you can replace Coach A with Coach B.

This story is meant to help the client recognize negative, unhelpful thoughts as they pop up (Coach A thoughts) and learn to develop more supportive, rational thinking (Coach B thoughts).

After telling the coaching story, go back to one of the Thought Records previously completed by the client at home, or discuss one completed in session together. Review the automatic thoughts and thinking errors that were identified. The next step is to evaluate the helpfulness of each thought. The following questions are suggested as prompts to help clients objectively evaluate these thoughts.

> *What is the evidence that this thought is true?*
>
> *Is there an alternate explanation?*
>
> *What is the worst thing that can happen?*
>
> *Has this situation unreasonably grown in importance?*
>
> *What would a good coach say about this situation?*
>
> *Have I done what I can to control it?*
>
> *If I were to do anything else, would this help or hinder the situation?*
>
> *Am I worrying excessively about this?*
>
> *What would a good friend say to me about this situation?*
>
> *What would I say to a good friend about this situation if he/she were going through it?*
>
> *Why is this statement a thinking error?*

Sometimes a client can maintain a vehement belief that the negative thought is true. One strategy is to acknowledge the part of it that seems true, but be sure that the intensity is appropriate and that the client is evaluating the worst-case scenario if it is true. Alternatively, it can be helpful to suggest that you return to this thought another time, as it is hard to work on it right now.

We now introduce a new five-column Thought Record with an additional column for formulating a rational response. The rational response is a statement that the client can say to himself to try to feel better about the situation. Keep in mind that we are not asking the client to overlook all negative aspects of his thoughts. The idea is to come up with a more balanced, objective, and helpful way of thinking about the situation.

Form: Thought Record

Time and Situation	Automatic Thoughts (what was going through your head?)	Mood and Intensity of Mood	Thinking Errors (match thoughts from list)	Rational Response

For example, consider Johnny's thoughts from the coaching story: "I am so stupid—I missed that ball. . . . I'll never become a good baseball player. . . . I'll always be a failure." The goal would be for him to acknowledge that he missed the ball on this one occasion but has caught others in the past (no magnification/minimization), to recognize that there are additional skills he can learn to help him become a better player (no fortune telling), and to see himself as having as good a chance as the next boy to become a ball player (no catastrophizing).

Potential Pitfalls

We have discussed several different types of thinking errors that can contribute to negative feelings. While it is important for the client to be familiar with the types of errors she may be making, remind her not to get stuck trying to find the exact type of error that corresponds with the thought. Thoughts may fit into more than one category, and often these categories of thinking errors overlap. The goal is for the client to recognize that the automatic thought might represent a thinking error, to understand why this is true, and, most important, to come up with a rational response.

For many clients, identifying a rational response may be tricky at first. Refer to the suggested questions (i.e., *what would you say to a friend who said this?*). Also, tell the client to keep in mind that thoughts and feelings about the situation may not completely change immediately after identifying a rational response. However, if he practices repeating the responses to himself, over time he will begin to replace the negative, automatic thoughts with more balanced ones.

Homework

■ Continue practicing skills learned in previous sections.

■ Use Thought Records or a notebook to list automatic thoughts, thinking errors, and rational responses for situations that occur during the following week.

- Read the form on developing a rational response.

- Complete Thought Records for at least two situations during the week.

  Remind the client that, with practice, he will feel more comfortable using his new skills and will begin to notice improvements. In session, identify situations to work on at home using the thought records. Also ask the client to consider any difficulties he may have completing this assignment, and problem-solve to minimize the chance that obstacles will emerge.

Case Vignette

T: Let's take a look at one of the Thought Records you completed this week and see if you can identify a rational response.

Time and Situation	Automatic Thoughts	Feelings and Intensity	Thinking Error	Rational Response
Wednesday 5:00 P.M. My boyfriend asked me to help him by making some phone calls, and I forgot to make them because I was surfing the Net for too long.	He's going to be so angry with me. He's going to break up with me. I'm so stupid. I always forget to do important things people ask of me.	Worried 100 Devastated, sad 100 Embarrassed 95	Jumping to conclusions Jumping to conclusions, catastrophizing	*He might be upset, but he will get over it. He doesn't usually stay mad for long. He loves many other aspects of me. This is just one mistake I made. Sometimes I forget to do things when I get distracted, but not always, and he knows I am attending this program to work on my ADHD.*

T: Start with the first thought: he's going to be so angry with me. What evidence do you have that supports or contradicts this thought?

C: Well, I know these calls were important. He had a really busy day and asked me to do him a favor by calling, so he will be mad. But, there have been other times when I forgot to do something and he was a little frustrated, but not really mad at me. So it's 50-50. He might get mad, but there is a chance he won't.

T: Good. Now, even if he is mad, is he going to break up with you? What's the evidence you have for that?

C: I get scared about this a lot. But, we have gotten into fights in the past, and even when it's a big one, he gets over it pretty quickly and doesn't hold a grudge. He tends to focus more on how to solve the problem. Plus, he does tell me all the time how much he loves me and wants to be with me. So he probably won't break up with me.

T: Great! So he may be mad, which will be hard for you, but it's pretty clear that he loves you and will stay with you. This is just a mistake you made. What about the last thought?

C: I get so mad at myself when I forget to do things. It's so humiliating.

T: Do these things happen every day, all day long?

C: Um, no. Maybe once a month.

T: And, you have been working extremely hard in this program so that you can learn new skills for managing your ADHD!

C: I have. And I have seen some changes. So has my boyfriend. He tells me how proud he is of me. He does know I'm trying hard.

T: Terrific. I understand it's hard for you when these things happen, but I think you can see now how these negative automatic thoughts can really intensify your feelings and make it difficult to problem solve and cope with the situation.

C: It's true. I can really see that now.

Form: Thought Record

Time and Situation	Automatic Thoughts (what was going through your head?)	Mood and Intensity of Mood	Thinking Errors (match thoughts from list)	Rational Response

Questions to help with rational response: *What is the evidence for the thought? Against the thought? Why is it the particular thinking error? Is there an alternate explanation? What is the worst thing that could happen? What would a good friend or good coach say? What would you say to a friend in a similar situation?*

Form: Adaptive Thinking II: Developing a Rational Response

The purpose of adaptive thinking is to help promote optimal thinking when you are feeling stressed. The steps that are involved can be achieved using the rest of the worksheet. Throughout the week when you are feeling stressed, sad, or overwhelmed, continue to list your thoughts in each situation. If you are anticipating a stressful situation or a task that is making you feel overwhelmed, write out your thoughts regarding this situation. If a situation has already passed and you find that you are thinking about it negatively, list your thoughts for this situation.

The **first column** is a description of the situation.

The **second column** is for you to list your thoughts during a stressful, overwhelming, or uncontrollable situation.

The **third column** is for you to write down what emotions you are having and what your mood is like when thinking these thoughts (e.g., depressed, sad, angry).

The **fourth column** is for you to see if your thoughts match the list of "thinking errors" These may include:

All-or-nothing thinking	Emotional reasoning
Overgeneralizations	"Should" statements
Jumping to conclusions: Fortune telling/ mind reading	Labeling and mislabeling
	Personalization
Magnification/minimization	Maladaptive thinking

The last column is for you to try to come up with a rational response to each thought, or to the most important negative thought. The rational response is a statement that you can say to yourself to try to feel better about the situation. Questions to help come up with this rational response can include:

What is the evidence that this thought is true?

Is there an alternate explanation?

What is the worst thing that can happen?

Has this situation unreasonably grown in importance?

What would a good coach say about this situation?

Have I done what I can do to control it?

If I were to do anything else, would this help or hinder the situation?

Am I worrying excessively about this?

What would a good friend say to me about this situation?

What would I say to a good friend about this situation if he were going through it?

Why is this statement a thinking error?

Session 10 | *Rehearsal and Review of Adaptive Thinking Skills*

(Corresponds to Chapter 12 of the Client Workbook)

Materials Needed

- Symptom Severity Scale
- Copies of blank Thought Records

Session Outline

- Set agenda
- Review Symptom Severity Scale
- Review medication adherence
- Review homework from previous modules
- Review Thought Records completed at home
- Identify additional situations that might require adaptive thinking for home practice
- Evaluate client's need to complete the Procrastination module
- Assign homework

Set Agenda

Remember that it is important to begin each session by setting an agenda to maintain a structured focus on treatment for ADHD and prepare the client for what lies ahead in the upcoming session. Use the session outline for your agenda.

Review of Symptom Severity Scale

Each week, the client completes the ADHD self-report symptom checklist at the beginning of the session. Review the total score and engage the client in a discussion about symptoms that have improved and those that are still problematic. It is helpful to keep all checklists organized in the client's file so that you may review previous scores as needed.

Score: _____

Date: _____

Review of Medication Adherence

Each week the client records his prescribed dosage of medication and indicates the number of doses that were missed during the week. Assist the client in identifying triggers for missed doses, such as distractibility, running out of medication, or thoughts about not wanting/needing to take medication. Problem-solve as necessary to increase adherence.

Prescribed doses per week: _____

Doses missed this week: _____

Triggers for missed doses: _____

_____

_____

Review of Previous Modules

Like the other sessions, this one includes a review of the client's progress implementing skills from each of the previous modules. It is important to acknowledge the successes she has achieved and to problem-solve around any difficulties she may be having. Repetition of new skills is critical for individuals with ADHD and will maximize gains made in treatment and increase the likelihood of sustaining improvement. At this point, we hope, the organization, planning and distractibility skills will have become automatic for the client. Some have more difficulty than others establishing new habits, so be sure to look out for problems your client may be having.

Review: Tools for Organization and Planning

- Calendar for managing appointments
- Notebook for recording a to-do list
- Notebook for breaking tasks down into subtasks
- Notebook for managing and prioritizing multiple tasks
- Strategies for problem-solving and developing an action plan
- Triage and filing systems

Review: Strategies for Managing Distractibility

- Breaking tasks down to match duration of attention span and taking breaks between tasks
- Utilizing distractibility delay
- Removing distractions from environment
- Identifying a specific place for each object
- Distractibility reminders (dots and alarm): "Am I doing what I am supposed to be doing?"

Review: Adaptive Thinking

- Using the Thought Record to identify and label automatic thoughts
- Identifying a rational response

Homework Review

In this session, review Thought Records the client completed at home and discuss any difficulties he may be having with adaptive thinking. If necessary, complete a new Thought Record to review these skills. If the client has not completed any at home, review the rationale behind homework in CBT, and emphasize that improvement is made only with continued practice. Assist the client in problem-solving around doing home practice.

Review: Strategies for Developing Adaptive Thinking

At this point, work with the client to identify any new situations that may require adaptive thinking. Patterns of negative thoughts or important themes may have emerged from prior homework assignments. Remind the client to refer to the handouts on adaptive thinking and sample Thought Records if she feels stuck. We also reiterate that initially, it is helpful to write out the five columns in the Thought Record. However, ultimately this process will take place in the client's mind. With practice, she will learn to spot unhelpful automatic thoughts as they emerge and will be able to come up with a rational response to feel better about the situation. When necessary, the client can always write out the Thought Record and review the handouts.

We suggest using this session to review an additional problematic situation and to complete a Thought Record in full for this situation.

Planning for Future Treatment

A hearty congratulations to your client is warranted!! He has now completed the core elements of cognitive-behavioral therapy for ADHD. Review the "goal list" that was completed at the beginning of his treatment to determine whether to begin the optional module on procrastination or do more review work on modules that have already been completed. The skills that have already been taught can be easily applied to the area of procrastination, which is detailed in the next chapter.

Potential Pitfalls

Your client has done a lot of work to get to this point! He may feel like taking a break or may believe that he has done enough work and will no longer have any difficulties related to ADHD. The most important message to emphasize is *practice, practice, practice!* This will ensure that newly learned skills become permanent. Your client's effort will continue to pay off.

Homework

- Continue practicing skills learned in previous sections.
- Continue to use the notebook and cognitive techniques for situations involving stress.

In session, remember to discuss any of the client's anticipated problems completing the homework.

Case Vignette

T: Congratulations! You've done a terrific job using the Thought Records to break down difficult situations and understand how negative thoughts can contribute to feeling badly in the situation. Let's review the goal list that was completed at the beginning of treatment and evaluate what would be helpful to work on next. It looks like you were feeling really overwhelmed by paperwork and organization and that you had problems with procrastination.

C: Right. I could never keep my bills straight and would get so anxious that I just couldn't deal. I've had to pay a lot of late fees because of this.

T: How are you doing with the organization strategies we've been working on?

C: Much better. I now have a system for filing my current bills and paying them each month. But I still sometimes try to avoid it when I get overwhelmed.

T: So you are still having some difficulties with procrastination. Perhaps we should spend some time working on the procrastination chapter.

C: I don't know. I feel like I have done a lot of work already. I've been coming here every week for several months now. I think that should be enough.

T: You're feeling like you've already put in your time to work on skills. I'm really glad you mention that. Actually, a lot of people feel that way. But here's the catch. You've been struggling with ADHD for many years, and have worked quite hard for three months, but it takes consistent practice to maintain the gains that you have made. You've mentioned a number of difficulties that have improved during the program—remembering important appointments, getting your work done on time, and being able to read without getting distracted. You can continue to improve if you keep practicing your CBT skills. When you think about it, it really takes only about 15 minutes a day at most to do homework, and the tradeoff is enormous!

C: Well, that is true. It just seems unfair. Other people don't have to worry about these things.

T: Others may not struggle with ADHD, but most people struggle in some area. Remember, we talked about the fact that you can't change the fact that you have ADHD, which can be hard to accept, but you can minimize the impact it has on your life by utilizing your CBT skills.

C: Yeah, I just have to remind myself of that.

T: You can. If you make it a habit to practice a little bit each day, it will become much easier! I know you can do it.

Module 4
Additional Skills

Session 11 | *Application of Skills to Procrastination*

(Corresponds to Chapter 13 of the Client Workbook)

Materials Needed

- Symptom Severity Scale
- Form: Pros and Cons of Procrastination
- Form: Thought Record

Session Outline

- Set agenda
- Review Symptom Severity Scale
- Review medication adherence
- Review home practice of previously learned skills
- Discuss the attractive aspects of procrastination
- Teach client to anticipate the negative consequences of procrastination
- Adapt the pros and cons (motivational exercise) to procrastination
- Introduce techniques for problem-solving around procrastination
- Explain how to use adaptive thinking skills for managing procrastination
- Identify areas for home practice

Set Agenda

It is important to begin each session by setting an agenda. Review the session outline with the client.

Review Symptom Severity Scale

Each week the client completes the ADHD self-report symptom checklist at the beginning of the session. Review the total score, and engage the client in a discussion about symptoms that have improved and those that are still problematic. It is helpful to keep all checklists organized in the client's file so that you may review previous scores as needed.

Score: _____

Date: _____

Review of Medication Adherence

Each week the client records her prescribed dosage of medication and indicates the number of doses that were missed during the week. Assist the client in identifying triggers for missed doses, such as distractibility, running out of medication, or thoughts about not wanting/needing to take medication. Problem-solve as necessary to increase adherence.

Prescribed doses per week: _____

Doses missed this week: _____

Triggers for missed doses: _____

_____

_____

Review Homework From Previous Modules

Each session also begins with a review of clients' progress implementing skills from each of the previous modules. It is important to acknowledge successes and to problem-solve any difficulties they may be having.

Review: Tools for Organization and Planning

- Calendar for managing appointments
- Notebook for recording a to-do list

- Notebook for breaking tasks down into subtasks

- Notebook for managing and prioritizing multiple tasks

- Strategies for problem-solving and developing an action plan

- Triage and filing systems

Review: Strategies for Reducing Distractibility

- Breaking tasks down to match duration of attention span and taking breaks between tasks

- Utilizing distractibility delay

- Removing distractions from the environment

- Identifying a specific place for each important object

- Distractibility reminders (dots and alarm): "Am I doing what I am supposed to be doing?"

Review: Adaptive Thinking

- Using Thought Records to identify negative thoughts

- Reviewing list of thinking errors

- Using Thought Records to create balanced, helpful thoughts

Introduction to Procrastination

Many individuals with ADHD have struggled with procrastination for quite some time, although many do not realize that ADHD can contribute to procrastination. In this chapter you will review your client's history with procrastination and try to identify the areas in which it has been most problematic. Some examples might include making phone calls, starting new tasks, applying for jobs, organizing papers, or getting daily projects done. Your goal in the session is to help the client identify especially difficult situations that lead to procrastination and to understand the cognitive and emotional factors that contribute to procrastination. Once your client discovers these reasons, he will be able to utilize more effective problem-solving strategies and decrease the interference of procrastination.

The Attractiveness of Procrastination

While procrastination can cause anxiety and anguish, there are also reasons why it *seems* desirable or easier to postpone tasks. Some reasons include:

- Perfectionism or fear of negative evaluation for a less-than-perfect product
- The difficulty of getting started started unless the time pressure is there
- The overwhelming nature of the issue
- The difficulty of finding a starting point
- The unattractive nature of tasks that require sustained effort
- The thought that it makes sense to wait for a period when there is enough time (this usually never comes)

Ask the client if any of these reasons sound familiar and prompt him to think about the reasons that seem to underlie procrastination for him. Determine if there any other reasons that are not included in the list. The attractiveness of procrastination is not always clear at a conscious level, but if the client thinks about it for a bit, some of the common reasons for procrastination will be recognized.

The Consequences of Procrastination

As discussed, procrastination can *appear* to be a good option for clients if it helps them avoid a negative feeling or if they *think* that the time/environment must be just right before they can begin a task. Unfortunately, these potential benefits are often outweighed by far more negative consequences. The goal of this section is to overemphasize the negative consequences so that they overpower the seemingly attractive aspects of procrastination. Some examples of negative consequences include:

- The stress of waiting until the last minute

- The fact that the task, which is unattractive in the first place, seems even worse when it is all-encompassing (waiting until the last minute means that one has to sacrifice other activities near the deadline)

- The risk of missing a deadline

- The tendency to feel worse about oneself afterward

- The fact that the final product is often not as good as it could have been

- The fact that ignoring the problem usually makes it even worse, and even harder to solve later

Ask your client if she recognizes any of these consequences. Has she experienced them? Prompt the client to think about how procrastination has had negative consequences in the course of her life. There may be other negative outcomes that are not listed here but that have been significant for the client.

Skill: Evaluating the Pros and Cons of Procrastination

In Session 1 of this treatment, a Pros/Cons worksheet was used to evaluate the merits and disadvantages of making changes in managing ADHD symptoms. This same technique is useful in helping clients understand the overall consequences of procrastination.

Remember that sometimes the short-term pros and cons differ from the long-term pros and cons, so be sure to evaluate both. This worksheet can be used with the client to objectively rate the pros and cons of procrastination. Unfortunately, it is sometimes difficult for clients to remember the pros and cons at the moment they are facing an overwhelming task. Explaining that, by taking the time now to practice reviewing the pros and the cons, they will be better able to remember the consequences in the moment when they are tempted to procrastinate.

Form: Evaluating the Pros and Cons of Procrastination

	Short-Term	Long-Term
Pros		
Cons		

Skill: Adapting Problem-Solving to the Issue of Procrastination

In Session 4 of treatment we introduced skills for problem-solving. When a task feels overwhelming, or a client is uncertain about where to begin, he is more likely to procrastinate. Breaking the task down into manageable steps will help avoid this. Remind your client that each step should feel completely doable. Ask him to do a "gut check." The gut response should be that the task feels absolutely doable. If it doesn't, the client should break the step down further. Alternatively, rather than attempting to work on the whole problem, he may want to target only one or two goals.

Another trap is to set unreasonable goals. Remind the client that each step should be realistic. The skills learned for managing distractibility will also be useful here. If your client knows that her attention span for working on unpleasant tasks is 15 minutes, then she should break down each step into goals that can be completed in this time frame.

Refer back to additional problem-solving worksheets completed in previous modules if necessary. These exercises can be done in the client's notebook.

Review: Breaking Large Tasks Down into Manageable Steps

1. **Choose a difficult or complex task from the to-do list.** List the steps that must be completed.

    This can be done using small note cards or plain paper. Ask questions such as "What is the first thing that you would need to do to make this happen?"

2. **For each step, make sure that it is manageable.**

    Have the client ask herself, "Is this something that I could realistically complete in one day?" and "Is this something that I would want to put off doing?" If the step itself is overwhelming, then it should be broken down into steps.

3. **List each individual step on the daily to-do list.**

In the module on adaptive thinking (Module 3), clients learned that their thoughts can play a powerful role in how they feel about a situation and can influence clients' actions in a situation. Negative automatic thoughts can also greatly contribute to procrastination. Using Thought Records will help clients create balanced, helpful thoughts that will decrease procrastination.

Remind your client about the five steps to completing the Thought Record.

1. List the situation that is contributing to procrastination.

2. List the automatic thoughts regarding the task or goal.

3. Identify the feelings connected to the thoughts.

4. Refer to the list of thinking errors to evaluate your thoughts.

5. Formulate rational responses to these thoughts.

Example

As we've emphasized throughout the manual, practicing new skills is essential if clients are ultimately to be able to use them easily in a given situation. Ask your client to think about a specific task or issue about which he has been procrastinating. Assist the client in using each of the skills listed for this task or issue. Use problem-solving to help break the task into manageable steps. Instruct the client to write down the steps in his notebook. Next, assist him in listing the automatic thoughts he is having about getting started. Finally, prompt him to identify the appropriate thinking errors and come up with helpful, rational responses.

Form: Thought Record

Time and Situation	Automatic Thoughts (what was going through your head?)	Mood and Intensity of Mood	Thinking Errors (match thoughts from list)	Rational Response

Potential Pitfalls

Although your client may have struggled with procrastination for many years, it is important to remind her that she can use the strategies she has learned to decrease the interference of procrastination. Even if she is unsure about whether the steps will help, encourage her to do an experiment! Instruct her to commit to using these skills each day for one month and see how well she does. Chances are, she will see the results quickly, and it will then be easier to practice the newly learned techniques.

Homework

- Plan a reasonable goal or two from the list of steps, and use strategies for avoiding procrastination as necessary.

- Help the client determine a way that she can reward herself upon completion of the goals.

- Review skills learned in previous sections, and note any questions or difficulties that client may be having.

Case Vignette

T: Let's think about how procrastination plays out for you and evaluate the pros and cons. Let's start with the short-term pros of procrastination

C: Well, I don't have to do the task I'm trying to avoid.

T: True. What else?

C: I can do something more fun like go out with my friends or play Nintendo.

T: I see. There are more enjoyable, attractive activities that you'd rather be doing. What are some of the long-term pros?

C: Hmmm. I'm not sure I can think of any other than what I've already mentioned. So the short-term pros are also the long-term pros?

T: Isn't that interesting. How about the short-term cons?

C: I always feel guilty and anxious when I know there is something I need to do and am avoiding doing it. That makes me feel tense, and then I usually get a migraine and get really irritable. My girlfriend hates when I get like that and sometimes says she won't see me until I finish whatever I need to do so I'll stop being so grouchy.

T: So even though it seems that you get to do more enjoyable activities when you're not doing the avoided tasks, you really suffer emotionally and physically, and you aren't able to spend as much time with your girlfriend as you could. What about the long-term consequences?

C: One time a different girlfriend broke up with me because I was always so irritable, and she knew it was because I was procrastinating. I guess I've also had problems at school. I usually wait until a few days before a test to make sure I have all the notes I need, and by then other people won't lend me their notes to copy because they need to use the notes for studying. I've always been a C student, but if I studied a little more I'd easily get at least a B.

T: That's too bad. Your relationships and school performance have really suffered. What do you realize when you really examine the short- and long-term pros and cons?

C: Of course, it's obvious! Procrastination creates more problems than it solves. If I could make some small changes, it could easily get better.

T: You're exactly right! Using the problem-solving skills can make it so much easier to complete tasks and avoid the cycle of procrastination. Why don't you do an experiment this week and see what happens when you use these skills?

C: Okay.

Session 12 *Relapse Prevention*

(Corresponds to Chapter 14 of the Client Workbook)

Materials Needed

- Symptom Severity Scale
- Form: Charting Progress
- Form: Examining the Value of Treatment Strategies
- Form: One-Month Review Sheet
- Form: Troubleshooting Difficulties

Session Outline

- Set agenda
- Review Symptom Severity Scale
- Review medication adherence
- Review treatment strategies and usefulness chart (included in this manual and in client workbook)
- Discussion of maintenance of gains
- Discussion of troubleshooting, using chart

Set Agenda

It is important to begin each session by setting an agenda. Review the session outline with the client.

Review Symptom Severity Scale

Each week the client completes the ADHD self-report symptom check-list at the beginning of the session. Review the total score and engage the client in a discussion about symptoms that have improved and those that are still problematic. It is helpful to keep all checklists organized in the client's file so that you may review previous scores as needed. If this session is a booster session and time has elapsed since the last session, have the client complete the checklist for the time period since the last session rather than the previous week.

Score: _____

Date: _____

Review of Medication Adherence

Each week the client records his prescribed dosage of medication and indicates the number of doses that were missed during the week. Assist the client in identifying triggers for missed doses, such as distractibility, running out of medication, or thoughts about not wanting/needing to take medication. Problem-solve as necessary to increase adherence.

Prescribed doses per week: _____

Doses missed this week: _____

Triggers for missed doses: _____

_____

_____

Ending Treatment but Maintaining Gains

The key to successful termination and relapse prevention for individuals with ADHD is persistent use of the skills. We recommend overemphasizing this point with clients. Most people hear the following phrase in almost every treatment session, as well as in the follow-up sessions:

The strategies and skills need to be practiced regularly so that they become more automatic.

In other words, the end of regular sessions of treatment signifies the starting point of the clients' own program of treatment, where they work to lock in and extend the skills and strategies that they have learned.

In order to help clients transition to this next phase of treatment—in which they take over the role as the therapist—it is important for them to recognize the nature of any benefits they have achieved.

One way to look at progress is to graph or table the ADHD rating scale scores from the program. If there are sudden gains in treatment—dramatic or significant reductions in a score on a given week—it is important to discuss what occurred that week that caused the change (i.e., finally purchased and started using the calendar book, finally started looking at the task list daily).

Form: Charting Progress

Session	Score
1	
2	
3	
4	
5	
6	
7	
8	
9	
10	
11	
12	
Other	

Examining What Was Valuable

In addition to attempting to recall which sessions had the most gains, we review the treatment strategies and determine how useful they are. This table is in the client's workbook and can be done at home and discussed in the session, or it can be done in the session itself as a discussion.

As the discussion progresses, the therapist can provide positive feedback regarding the approaches that worked and emphasize the importance of continuing to use them. If there are strategies that have not worked, these do not need to be continued. However, the therapist should also problem-solve any difficulties (e.g., any strategies that are no longer being used, or any that are not being done in the best possible way).

Maintaining Gains

An important distinction for clients to be aware of is the difference between a "setback" and a "relapse." We consider "setbacks" to be part of progress. Successful treatment does not mean that you will not have future difficulties with symptoms. For most conditions, symptoms can wax and wane over time.

Stress the idea that the key to maintaining treatment gains over the long run is to be ready for periods of increased difficulties. Explain that these periods are not signs that the treatment has failed. Instead, these periods are signals that the client needs to apply the skills. The client can use the form on page 144 to refresh the skills as needed. The purpose of the form is to remind the client of the importance of practicing skills and to help the client think through which strategies might be important for him to practice.

Talk with client about scheduling review session for herself. Discuss using the calendar to pick a time and date in one month.

Form: Examining the Value of Treatment Strategies

Please rate the usefulness of each strategy to you (0 = Didn't help at all, 100 = Was extremely important for me). Also, take some time to provide notes to yourself about why you think each strategy worked or didn't work to help you, and figure out which strategies might be most helpful for you to practice over the next month.

Treatment Strategies	Usefulness Ratings	Notes about Your Application/Usefulness of the Strategy
Review: Tools for Organization and Planning		
■ Calendar for managing appointments		
■ Notebook for recording a to-do list		
■ Notebook for breaking tasks down into subtasks		
■ Notebook for managing and prioritizing multiple tasks		
■ Strategies for problem-solving and developing an action plan		
■ Triage and filing systems		
Review: Strategies for Managing Distractibility		
■ Breaking tasks down to match duration of attention span and taking breaks between tasks		
■ Utilizing distractibility delay		
■ Using stimulus control for environment and removing distractions		
■ Using stimulus control for important objects and identify specific place for each		
■ Distractibility reminders (dots and alarm): "Am I doing what I am supposed to be doing?"		
Review: Adaptive Thinking		
■ Using Thought Records to identify negative thoughts		
■ Reviewing list of thinking errors		
■ Using Thought Records to create balanced, helpful thoughts		

1. What skills have you been practicing well?

2. Where do you still have troubles?

3. Can you place the troubles in one of the specific domains used in this treatment?

4. Have you reviewed the chapters most relevant to your difficulties? (Which chapters are these?)

5. Have you reviewed the table in which you recorded which skills were most helpful to you in the first phase of this treatment? Do you need to reapply these skills or strategies?

Troubleshooting Difficulties

It may also be helpful to match some of the symptoms the client is experiencing with some of the specific strategies used in treatment. Use the form that follows to help the client match specific symptoms with skills that were taught in the treatment sessions.

Finally, you may want to suggest that the client use the problem-solving forms in Chapter 6 to more carefully consider any difficulties with symptoms. Suggest that the client enlist the help of family and friends and/or schedule a booster session with you if these strategies are not effective in reducing the client's ADHD symptoms.

Termination

As with any therapy, spend some time processing termination with the client. Share your thoughts about how it was for you to work with the client, noting aspects of the treatment that were especially enjoyable for you (i.e., *"I know you really had doubts about being able to track all of your appointments in the calendar, and it was a pleasure for me to watch you work through that and get to the point now where you can't imagine not using your calendar daily"*).

Congratulate the client for all of the hard work that was put into completing this treatment program. It was demanding! However, we truly believe these skills can make a profound difference and help reduce the severity of ADH D symptoms. Remind the client one final time to *practice, practice, practice* the skills that were learned! Improvements will not magically maintain themselves. Only through continued use will they become automatic (refer to the vignettes in Sessions 1 and 10 if necessary).

Form: Troubleshooting Difficulties

Symptoms	Skills to Consider
Failing to give adequate attention to details/making careless mistakes in work or other activities	Recheck attention span and ability to break activities into units. Use cues (beeper, dots) as reminders of core responsibilities at hand.
Difficulty sustaining attention in tasks	Check management of space (are environments too distracting?).
Failing to listen when spoken to directly	Talk to others about finding optimal times for conversations, or use shorter units of talk.
Difficulty organizing tasks in terms of importance	Use notebook and rating system. Use triage and filing systems.
Procrastination	Use problem-solving and adaptive thinking.
Losing things necessary for tasks or activities	Use a single work area. Use triage and filing systems. Work with another person to reduce clutter.
Becoming easily distracted by extraneous stimuli	Manage environment, and use distractibility delay.
Being forgetful in daily activities	Use beeper system and to-do list, along with calendar.

References

Adler, L. A., & Chua, H. C. (2002). Management of ADHD in adults. *Journal of Clinical Psychiatry, 63* (Suppl. 12), 29–35.

American Psychiatric Association (1994). *Diagnostic and statistical manual of mental disorders* (4th ed.). Washington, DC: Author.

Barkley, R. A. (1998). *Attention-deficit hyperactivity disorder: A handbook for diagnosis and treatment* (2nd ed.). New York: Guilford Press.

Barkley, R. A., & Murphy, K. R. (1998). *Attention-deficit hyperactivity disorder: A clinical workbook* (2nd ed.). New York: Guilford Press.

Bellak, L., & Black, R.,B. (1992). Attention-deficit hyperactivity disorder in adults. *Clinical Therapeutics, 14,* 138–147.

Biederman, J., Faraone, S. V., Keenan, K., Steingard, R., & Tsuang, M. T. (1991). Familial association between attention deficit disorder and anxiety disorders. *American Journal of Psychiatry, 148,* 251–256.

Biederman, J., Farone, S. V., Keenan, K., Benjamin, J., Krifcher, B., Moore, C., Sprich, S., Ugaglia, K., Jellinek, M. S., Steingard, R., Spencer, T., Norman, D., Kolodny, R., Kraus, I., Perrin, J., Keller, M. B., & Tsuang, M. T. (1992). Further evidence for family genetic risk factors in attention deficit hyperactivity disorder: Patterns of comorbidity in probands and relatives in psychiatrically and pediatrically referred samples. *Archives of General Psychiatry, 49,* 728–738.

Biederman, J., Farone, S. V., Spencer, T., Wilens, T., Mick, E., & Lapey, K. A. (1994). Gender differences in a sample of adults with attention deficit hyperactivity disorder. *Psychiatry Research, 53,* 13–29.

Biederman, J., Farone, S. V., Spencer, T., Wilens, T., Norman, D., Lapey, K. A., Mick, E., Lehman, B. K., & Doyle, A. (1993). Patterns of comorbidity, cognition, and psychosocial functioning in adults with attention deficit hyperactivity disorder. *American Journal of Psychiatry, 150,* 1792–1798.

Biederman, J., Munir, K., Knee, D., Armentano, M., Autor, S., Waternaux, C., & Tsuang, M. (1987). High rate of affective disorders in probands with attention deficit disorder and in their relatives: A controlled family study. *American Journal of Psychiatry, 144,* 330–333.

Biederman, J., Munir, K., Knee, D., Habelow, W., Armentano, M., Autor, S., Hoge, S. K., & Watermaux, C. (1986). A family study of patients with attention deficit disorder and normal controls. *Journal of Psychiatric Research, 20*, 263–274.

Biederman, J., Wilens, T. E., Spencer, T. J., Farone, S., Mick, E., Ablon, J. S., & Keily, K. (1996). Diagnosis and treatment of adult attention-deficit/hyperactivity disorder. In M. H. Pollack, M. W. Otto, & J. F. Rosenbaum (Eds.), *Challenges in clinical practice*, pp. 380–407. New York: Guilford Press.

Cantwell, D. P. (1972). Psychiatric illness in the families of hyperactive children. *Archives of General Psychiatry, 27*, 414–417.

Craske, M. G., Barlow, D. H., & Meadows, E. A. (2000). *Mastery of your anxiety and panic (MAP-3)*. Boston: Graywind.

Farone, S.V., Biederman, J., Keenan, K., & Tsuang, M. T. (1991). A family-genetic study of girls with DSM-III attention deficit disorder. *American Journal of Psychiatry, 148*, 112–117.

Goodman, R. (1989). Genetic factors in hyperactivity account for about half of the explainable variance. *British Medical Journal, 298*, 1407–1408.

Goodman, R., & Stevenson, J. (1989) A twin study of hyperactivity: II. The etiological role of genes, family relationships and perinatal adversity. *Journal of Child Psychology and Psychiatry, 30*, 691–709.

Heimberg, R. H. (1991). *Cognitive-behavioral treatment of social phobia in a group: A treatment manual.* Unpublished manuscript available from author, Temple University, Philadelphia, PA.

Hope, D. A., Heimberg, R. H., Juster, H. R., & Turk, C. L. (2000). *Managing social anxiety: A cognitive-behavioral therapy approach.* Boulder, CO: Graywind.

Lahey, B. B., Piacentini, J. C., McBurnett, K., Stone, P., Hartdagen, S., & Hynd, G. (1988). Psychopathology in the parents of children with conduct disorder and hyperactivity. *Journal of the American Academy of Child and Adolescent Psychiatry, 27*, 163–170.

Linehan, M. (1993). *Cognitive-behavioral treatment of borderline personality disorder.* New York: Guilford Press.

McDermott, S. P. (2000). Cognitive therapy of adults with Attention-Deficit/Hyperactivity Disorder. In T. Brown (Ed.), *Attention deficit disorders and comorbidity in children, adolescents, and adults.* Washington, DC: American Psychiatric Press.

Morrison, J. R. (1980). Adult psychiatric disorders in parents of hyperactive children. *American Journal of Psychiatry, 137*, 825–837.

Morrison, J. R., & Stewart, M. A. (1973). The psychiatric status of the legal families of adopted hyperactive children. *Archives of General Psychiatry, 28*, 888–891.

Murphy, K., & Barkley, R. A. (1996a). Attention deficit hyperactivity disorder adults: Comorbidities and adaptive impairments. *Comprehensive Psychiatry, 37*, 393–401.

Murphy, K., & Barkley, R. A. (1996b). Prevalence of DSM-IV symptoms of ADHD in adult licensed drivers: Implications for clinical practice. *Journal of Attention Disorders, 1*, 147–161.

Murphy, K. R., & Gordon, M. (1998). Assessment of adults with ADHD. In R. Barkley (Ed.), *Attention deficit hyperactivity disorder: A handbook for diagnosis and treatment* (2nd ed.). New York: Guilford Press.

Otto, M. (2000). Stories and metaphors in cognitive-behavior therapy. *Cognitive and Behavioral Practice, 69*, 166–172.

Otto, M. W., Jones, J. C., Craske, M. G., & Barlow, D. H. (1996). *Stopping anxiety medication: Panic control therapy for benzodiazepine discontinuation (therapist guide).* San Antonio, TX: Psychological Corporation.

Persons, J. B. (1989). *Cognitive therapy in practice: A case formulation approach.* New York: Norton.

Ratey, J. J., Greenberg, M. S., Bemporad, J. R., & Lindem, K. J. (1992). Unrecognized attention-deficit hyperactivity disorder in adults presenting for outpatient psychotherapy. *Journal of Child and Adolescent Psychopharmacology, 2*, 267–275.

Safer, D. (1973). A familial factor in minimal brain dysfunction. *Behavior Genetics, 3*, 175–186.

Safren, S. A., Otto, M. W., Sprich, S., Perlman, C. L., Wilens, T. E., & Biederman, J. (in press). Cognitive-behavioral therapy for ADHD in medication-treated adults with continued symptoms. *Behaviour Research and Therapy.*

Shekim, W. O., Asarnow, R. F., Hess, E., Zaucha, K., & Wheeler, N. (1990). A clinical demographic profile of a sample of adults with attention deficit hyperactivity disorder, residual state. *Comprehensive Psychiatry, 31*, 416–425.

Spencer, T., Biederman, J., Wilens, T. E., & Farone, S. V. (1998). Adults with attention-deficit/hyperactivity disorder: A controversial diagnosis. *Journal of Clinical Psychiatry, 59* (Suppl. 7), 59–68.

Spencer, T., Biederman, J., Wilens, T. E., & Farone, S. V. (2002). Overview and neurobiology of attention-deficit/hyperactivity disorder. *Journal of Clinical Psychiatry, 63* (Suppl. 12), 2–9.

Spitzer, R. L., & Williams, J. B. W. (1985). Classfication in psychiatry. In H. I. Kaplan & B. J. Sadock (Eds.), *Comprehensive textbook of psychiatry* (4th ed.) (pp. 591–613). Baltimore, MD: Williams & Wilkins.

Sprich, S., Biederman, J., Crawford, M. H., Mundy, E., & Farone, S. V. (2000). Adoptive and biological families of children and adolescents with ADHD. *Journal of the American Academy of Child and Adolescent Psychiatry, 11*, 1432–1437.

Stevenson, J., Pennington, B. F., Gilger, J. W., DeFries, J. C., & Gillis, J. J. (1993). Hyperactivity and spelling disability: testing for shared genetic aetiology. *Journal of Child Psychology and Psychiatry, 49*, 728–738.

Szatmari, P., Boyle, M., & Offord, D. (1993). Familial aggregation of emotional and beahvioral problems of childhood in the general population. *American Journal of Psychiatry, 150*, 1398–1403.

Wender, P. H. (1998). Pharmacotherapy of attention-deficit/hyperactivity disorder in adults. *Journal of Clinical Psychiatry, 59* (Suppl. 7), 76–79.

Wilens, T. E., Biederman, J., & Spencer, T. J. (1998a). Pharmacotherapy of attention deficit hyperactivity disorder in adults. *CNS Drugs, 9*, 347–356.

Wilens, T. E., Spencer, T. J., & Biederman, J. (1998b). Pharmacotherapy of adult ADHD. In R. A. Barkley (Ed.), *Attention deficit hyperactivity disorder: A handbook for diagnosis and treatment* (2nd ed.) (pp. 592–606). New York: Guilford Press.

Wilens, T. E., McDermott, S. P., Biederman, J., Abrantes, A., Hahesy, A., & Spencer, T. J. (1999). Cognitive therapy in the treatment of adults with ADHD: A systematic chart review of 26 cases. *Journal of Cognitive Psychotherapy: An International Quarterly, 13*, 215–227.

Wilens, T. E., Spencer, T. J., & Biederman, J. (2002a). A review of the pharamcotherapy of adults with attention-deficit/hyperactivity disorder. *Journal of Attentional Disorders, 5*, 189–202.

Wilens, T. E., Biederman, J., & Spencer, T. J. (2002b). Attention deficit/hyperactivity disorder across the lifespan. *Annual review of medicine, 53*, 113–131

Zametkin, A. J., & Liotta, W. (1998). The neurobiology of attention-deficit/hyperactivity disorder. *Journal of Clinical Psychiatry, 59* (Suppl. 7), 17–23.

About the Authors

Steven A. Safren, Ph.D., is the Associate Director of the Cognitive-Behavioral Therapy Program and the Director of the Behavioral Medicine Service at Massachusetts General Hospital, as well as an Assistant Professor of Psychology at Harvard Medical School. Dr. Safren maintains a clinical practice treating clients with cognitive-behavioral therapy in addition to his involvement with training and research. Dr. Safren was the principal investigator of a two-year initial study of CBT for adult ADHD funded by the National Institute of Mental Health (NIMH) and is the principal investigator of a five-year NIMH study to evaluate its efficacy. He has authored more than 40 publications in the areas of cognitive-behavioral therapy, psychopathology, and their application to a variety of clinical problems in adults. In addition to his focus on adult ADHD, Dr. Safren works on the development and testing of interventions related to medical problems such as HIV. This work is also funded by the National Institutes of Health.

Carol A. Perlman, Ph.D., received her doctorate in clinical psychology from the University of Miami in Coral Gables, Florida, and is a Clinical Assistant in Psychology at Massachusetts General Hospital (MGH), an Instructor in Psychology at Harvard Medical School, and Project Director at the Harvard University Department of Psychology. She is a cognitive-behavioral therapist who specializes in the treatment of mood disorders, anxiety disorders, and adult ADHD. Dr. Perlman served as a therapist for the initial study of CBT for adult ADHD and is a co-investigator and therapist for the efficacy study. Dr. Perlman is also involved in clinical research examining the efficacy of cognitive-behavioral therapy for posttraumatic stress disorder and bipolar disorder. She is also the project director for a study of memory of childhood sexual abuse and treats clients in the MGH outpatient clinic.

Susan Sprich, Ph.D., received her doctorate in clinical psychology from the State University of New York at Albany. She is a Clinical Assistant in Psychology at Massachusetts General Hospital (MGH) and an Instructor in Psychology at Harvard Medical School. She is the Project Director for a five-year study of CBT for adult ADHD funded by NIMH. She is also involved in clinical research in the treatment of PTSD, trichotillomania, and other anxiety and mood disorders. She has authored more than 15 publications in the areas of ADHD and anxiety disorders in children and adults. Dr. Sprich conducts cognitive-behavioral therapy with clients with mood disorders, anxiety disorders, and ADHD through the Cognitive-Behavioral Therapy Program at MGH and in private practice.

Michael W. Otto, Ph.D., helped develop the Cognitive-Behavior Therapy Program at Massachusetts General Hospital (MGH), serving as director of the program and Associate Professor of Psychology at Harvard Medical School until leaving MGH in 2004 to become Professor of Psychology at Boston University. Clinically, Dr. Otto has specialized in the treatment of anxiety and mood disorders and has developed clinical research programs for the treatment of panic disorder, posttraumatic stress disorder, social phobia, bipolar disorder, psychotic disorders, substance dependence, and medication discontinuation in clients with panic disorder. Dr. Otto's research activities are closely tied to his clinical interests and target investigations of the etiology and treatment of anxiety, mood, and substance-use disorders. Of particular interest to him is the development and testing of new treatments, including the modification of treatment packages for novel populations (e.g., Cambodian refugees). He is a federally funded investigator and has published more than 170 articles, chapters, and books spanning these research interests.